Jack Jouett: Revolutionary Rider

The Ride that Saved Virginia

and

The American Revolution

by

Judy Bloodgood Bander

For Matt — I hope you enjoy this history
Judy Bander
7/21/17

> Without Jouett's warning, not one man
> of those in town would have escaped.
> —Benjamin Harrison

2014
Woodside Publishers

Located at Courthouse Square, Charlottesville, VA

This book is dedicated to the one who helps make my materials presentable and ready to be published, my husband Morris. From Woodside, Pennsylvania to Only Forever.

ISBN 978-1-4675-9030-3

CAPTAIN JACK JOUETT, JR.
1754 – 1822
BEGAN HIS PERILOUS RIDE ON HORSEBACK NEAR THIS POINT, CUCKOO TAVERN, TO MONTICELLO, BETWEEN MIDNIGHT AND DAWN ON JUNE 4, 1781, WHICH SAVED GOVERNOR THOMAS JEFFERSON AND THE VIRGINIA GENERAL ASSEMBLY IN SESSION AT CHARLOTTESVILLE FROM CAPTURE BY THE BRITISH UNDER LIEUTENANT COLONEL BANASTRE TARLETON, THUS PROTECTING THE AUTHOR OF THE DECLARATION OF INDEPENDENCE AS WELL AS CONTRIBUTING TO THE LIBERTY OF HIS COUNTRY. MAY HIS MEMORY LIVE FOREVER IN THE HEARTS OF HIS COUNTRYMEN. THIS BOULDER, FROM THE LAND OF CUCKOO, WAS PLACED FIRST IN 1926 BY THE PEOPLE OF THE VILLAGE AND LOUISA COUNTY AT A SITE APPROXIMATELY 40 FEET DISTANT GIVEN BY DR. EUGENE PENDLETON WHOSE FAMILY HAS OWNED "CUCKOO" SINCE 1815. IT WAS RELOCATED HERE IN 1968.

TABLETS ERECTED IN 1926 AND 1968 BY
THE JACK JOUETT CHAPTER VIRGINIA
NATIONAL SOCIETY DAUGHTERS OF
THE AMERICAN REVOLUTION

Acknowledgments

Thanks to Donna Fontaine, who bought my first book, *No Borrowed Glory*, at Patrick Henry's home and brought it back to Westside Elementary School in Isle of Wight County, Virginia. Because of her, my stories and research have found an outlet to many teachers and students in Isle of Wight County and beyond.

Anne Evans, Coordinator of Social Studies for Charlottesville Public Schools, made *No Borrowed Glory* available to teachers throughout Virginia. Her encouragement helped Jack Jouett have a new, exciting story.

Gary Persinger provided information and pictures about the plaque at Trinity Church in Staunton and its Harouf chair. Elaine Taylor of the Louisa County Museum and Steven Meeks, President of the Albemarle Charlottesville Historical Society, offered Jack Jouett resources for this project. Thanks to Jim Petrovits, owner of the Silver Thatch Inn, for generously sharing his time and home, especially the Hessian Room. The history of the building is special.

Thanks to Woodford County (Ky.) Museum for permission to use the Jack Jouett silhouette. Sunny Agee connected me with Diane Inman, Regent of the Jack Jouett Chapter of the Daughters of the American Revolution.

Thanks also go to Carolyn Coffman and Frances Robb for their proofreading skills. I thank Jean L. Cooper for her work in the final editing of the manuscript. And, to my friends who encouraged me to write an interesting and informative story. JBB

Jack Jouett: Revolutionary Rider

(Title Unknown)

"Hearken good people; awhile abide
And hear of stout Jack Jouett's ride;
How he rushed his steed, nor stopped nor stayed
Till he warned the people of Tarleton's Raid.

The moment his warning note was rehearsed
The State Assembly was quickly dispersed.

In their haste to escape they did not stop
Until they had crossed the mountain top.
And upon the other side come down
To resume their sessions in Staunton town.

His panting steed he spurred,
In haste to carry the warning word
To that greatest statesman of any age,
The immortal Monticello Sage.

Here goes to thee, Jack Jouett!
Lord keep thy mem'ry green;
You made the greatest ride, sir
That ever yet was seen."

This poem appeared in *Jack Jouett of Albemarle: The Paul Revere of Virginia* by Jennie Thornley Grayson. It was written sometime before October 1909 according to Jeanmarie Andrews.* Unfortunately the name of the poet has been lost. Used by permission of the Jack Jouett Chapter of Daughters of the American Revolution.

* "Another Famous Ride" *Early American Life*, April 2013.

Counties Involved in this Book

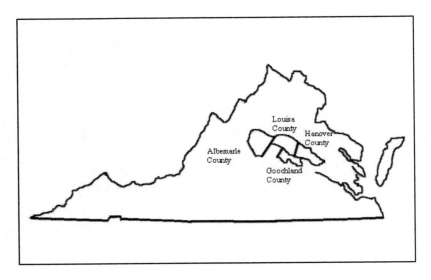

This map shows counties where action took place during the time period studied in the book. Tarleton's ride started in Hanover County outside of Richmond. He rode through Louisa County and into Albemarle County where Monticello is located. On his ride back to meet Cornwallis, he went through the southern part of Goochland County and raided Rock Castle located on the James River. That river forms a southern boundary of Goochland County.

Table of Contents

Maps and Illustrations

Significant Locations along Tarleton's Raid

Ground Squirrel Bridge is a landmark on Rt. 33 in Hanover County. The bridge goes over the South Anna River. Tarleton crossed the bridge on his way to Charlottesville.
Latitude 37.7601437N – Longitude 77.6119324W

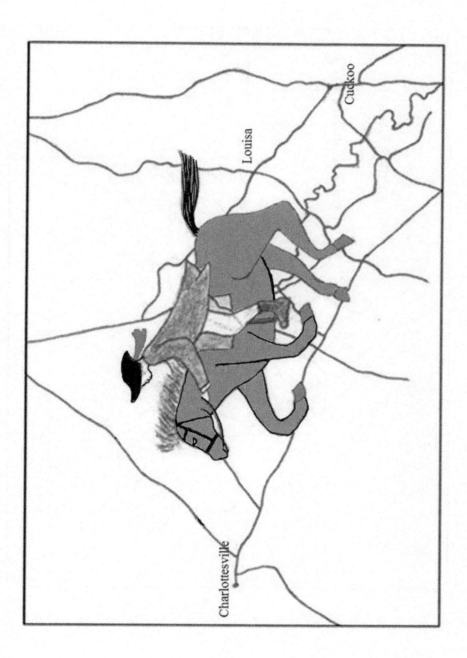

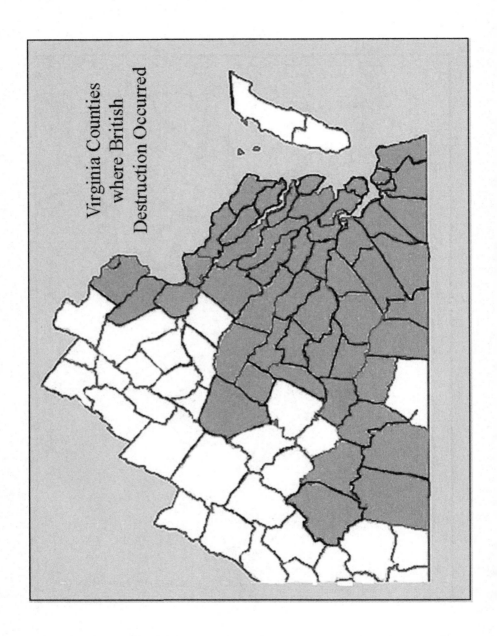

Virginia Counties where British Destruction Occurred

Cornwallis Brought the War to Virginia

Virginia was the largest and most populous of the thirteen colonies.[1] It also had the least experience with war and enemy armies. The colony had been furnishing troops, horses and other supplies to the fighting in the north.[2] As the war dragged on, depleting the supplies in the northern theater, Virginia's burgeoning foodstuff trade increasingly became the mainstay of armies stationed around the country. Virginians began to dream of commercial enterprises that once had been the preserve of Boston, New York and Philadelphia.[3]

General Lord Charles Cornwallis was frustrated fighting in the Carolinas, where he won battles but lost many soldiers. When his army moved on, those territories returned to their patriotic loyalties. On April 10, 1781, Cornwallis wrote his commanding officer, General Sir Henry Clinton, that he thought the key to winning the war was to control Virginia. He said he would like to see the Chesapeake become the seat of the war, even if that meant moving troops out of New York City and bringing them to Virginia.[4] He wrote to British General William Phillips in Petersburg, Virginia, saying "...bringing our whole force into Virginia might lead to victory in the war."[5]

Cornwallis believed until Virginia was conquered, they could not hold the more southern provinces, and without Virginia's support the southern colonies would fall without much difficulty.[6]

Eight days later (April 18), Cornwallis wrote to Lord George Germain[7] in Britain saying that Virginia was supplying reinforcements to the Carolinas, and British small raids and short occupations did not frighten the powerful state.[8] He believed the war must go to Virginia in full force.

JACK JOUETT'S RIDE

On 4 June 1781, John "Jack" Jouett Jr. arrived at the Albemarle County Courthouse to warn the Virginia legislature of approaching British troops. The state government under Governor Thomas Jefferson had retreated from Richmond to reconvene in Charlottesville because of the threat of British invasion during the Revolutionary War. Jouett had spotted Colonel Banastre Tarleton and his 180 dragoons and 70 cavalrymen 40 miles east at Cuckoo Tavern, and rode through the night to reach here by dawn. Jouett's heroic ride, which allowed Jefferson and all but seven of the legislators to escape, was later recognized by the Virginia General Assembly, which awarded him a sword and a pair of pistols.

DEPARTMENT OF HISTORIC RESOURCES, 1998

Located at Courthouse Square, Charlottesville, Virginia

Latitude 38.031851N – Longitude 78.477152W

Jack Jouett

Captain John (Jack) Jouett, Jr., born on December 7, 1754, in Albemarle County, was twenty-six years old on June 3, 1781, when he made his famous ride.

Jack was six feet, four inches tall, weighed at least two hundred twenty pounds and was a strong man. He was an excellent horseman. Having grown up in the area around Louisa County and Charlottesville, he knew that country well.[9]

In the spring of 1779, both Jack and his father signed The Albemarle Declaration, adding their names to the over two hundred other signatures from Albemarle County. The document informed anyone who read it that those men renounced allegiance to King George III and any future rulers of England. Their allegiance was to the state of Virginia.

Thomas Jefferson had recruited Jack to join Virginia's 16th Regiment with a bounty the state used to attract new recruits. Jack received £51[10] on April 15, 1777.[11] At the time, £45 was equal to about $150 today. By September 1780, when Jefferson had been Governor for fifteen months, Virginia, like other states, had a problem recruiting men to serve. It was even more difficult to get men to fight outside the state. Any volunteer who would sign up to serve until the end of the war was promised a bounty of $12,000 and three hundred acres of land located in western Virginia.[12]

John Jouett, Sr., had four sons, Matthew, Jack, William and Robert,[13] who fought in the Revolutionary War.[14] Matthew died at the Battle of Brandywine (September 11, 1777) in Pennsylvania.[15] Jack later named a son Matthew after his deceased brother.

3

John Jouett, Sr., sold considerable beef and other supplies to the Continental Army from his Louisa County farm, even though he could have made more money by selling to the British as some other farmers did.

In 1742, Jack's grandfather, Matthew Jouett, had opened an ordinary (tavern) in his house near the present town of Louisa. John, Sr., married Mourning Glenn Harris. She was a member of a prominent family of Brown's Cove, Albemarle County.[16] John, Sr., at one time owned the Cuckoo Tavern. According to Albemarle historian Edgar Woods, John, Sr., later purchased one hundred acres in Charlottesville, and before the war had built and kept the Swan Tavern located on the east side of the Courthouse Square.[17] Many members of the General Assembly, including Jefferson, met and stayed there when the Assembly moved to town.[18] When Jack rode to Charlottesville after warning Jefferson, he went to the Swan Tavern, knowing some members of the General Assembly were staying there.

The Jouett family was Huguenot and had originally come from France. Jack's great grandfather, Jean Jouett, moved to Virginia from Rhode Island.[19]

1781
Cuckoo, Virginia
The Beginning of a Revolutionary Ride

Virginia State Route 33 intersects and forms a triangle with State Route 522 in Louisa County. Near this triangle is Cuckoo. Route 33 continues west through the town of Louisa and then northwest. There was at least one building located in Cuckoo when Jack Jouett began his famous ride on June 3, 1781. That building was a tavern. Early in its existence, it may have been named Winston's Ordinary. Travelers stopped there to rest for the night on trips between Charlottesville and Fredericksburg or Richmond. John Jouett, Sr., owned the tavern for a time; however, he sold it to Sackville King on December 13, 1773.

The name of Sackville King's Ordinary was later changed to the Cuckoo Tavern because it had a cuckoo clock that was quite a novelty and was a tourist attraction. According to legend, the area was named Cuckoo after the clock that hung in the tavern.[20]

In 1815, Colonel Edmund Pendleton bought the land and three years later had a brick home built. The home was named "Cuckoo" after the tavern. Today there is a historical monument with a plaque commemorating Jack Jouett's ride located on the site. It was placed there in 1926 by Louisa County and relocated by the Jack Jouett, Jr., Chapter of the Daughters of the American Revolution in 1968.[21]

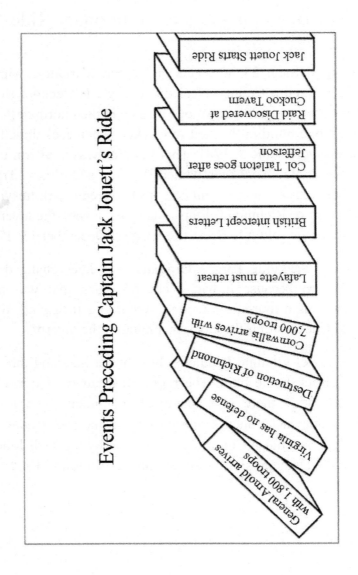

Events Preceding Captain Jack Jouett's Ride

- Jack Jouett Starts Ride
- Raid Discovered at Cuckoo Tavern
- Col. Tarleton goes after Jefferson
- British intercept Letters
- Lafayette must retreat
- Cornwallis arrives with 7,000 troops
- Destruction of Richmond
- Virginia has no defense
- General Arnold arrives with 1,800 troops

Events preceding Captain Jack Jouett's Ride

Events that led to Jack Jouett's desperate ride began when British General Benedict Arnold and his 1,800 redcoats arrived in the state on January 1, 1781. Unlike other raids in the past when the British did not remain any length of time, the enemy came to Virginia to stay until they won the war. For the next ten months, Virginians were constantly fighting for their survival. The state was completely unprepared for this invasion.

The state lacked sufficient militia to protect its citizens, their homes, livestock and especially their well-bred horses. This terrible lack of manpower was partly due to the capture of 5,500 American officers and men at the surrender of Charleston, South Carolina, on May 12, 1780. Added to that loss was the virtual annihilation of the remaining Virginia Line seventeen days later at Waxhaw, South Carolina. At the end of the battle British Colonel Banastre Tarleton's men massacred many wounded Virginians after they had surrendered.[22]

General Washington had written in his diary that "scarce any State in the Union has, at this hour, an eighth part of its quota [of militia] in the field. I can see little prospect of ever getting more than half of those men." He added that "instead of having the prospects of a glorious offensive campaign before us, we have a bewildered and gloomy defensive One."[23]

On May 20, 1781, five months after Arnold arrived in Virginia, Cornwallis entered Petersburg from North Carolina. He joined forces with Arnold and took command of recently deceased (May 13) General William Phillips' army. On May 24, British General Alexander Leslie arrived in Portsmouth with reinforcements for

Cornwallis from New York.[24] This gave the British about 7,000 troops. Cornwallis intended to conquer Virginia and cripple the American war effort.

American patriot presence in Virginia in early spring consisted of General Marquis de Lafayette's 1,200 soldiers, who were too few and too poorly trained and equipped to hinder the British.

The Virginia General Assembly planned to call out thousands of new militia to stop the British invasion.[25] The British considered men like Thomas Jefferson, writer of that "seditious document" the Declaration of Independence,[26] and members of the General Assembly as legitimate military targets.[27]

A foreshadow of events:

Moving the State Capital

In May 1779, the Virginia legislature (General Assembly) passed the Act for the Removal of the Seat of Government from Williamsburg to Richmond. It said Richmond was more safe and central than any other town. Richmond had deep water for the transportation of goods. It had been a tobacco inspection station since 1730.

The first Session met in Richmond on May 1, 1780. Because the state business in Richmond was conducted in an old warehouse, the building was not easily recognized as the seat of government.[28]

The Assembly did not know at that time they would have to move to a tavern owned and operated by John Jouett, Sr. The Jouett family and Thomas Jefferson knew each other as he often dined at the Swan Tavern.[29] Neither family knew that a year later, on June 11, 1782,

John Jouett, Sr., would have to present the House of Delegates with a petition to compensate him for damages to his house (the Swan Tavern) that occurred when the General Assembly used it for their business meetings. They had pulled down a partition and cut doors so all of the Assembly could fit inside.[30]

Sir Henry Clinton
Picture courtesy of http://commons.wikimedia.org/wiki/
File:SirHenryClinton_BestLo.jpg

Lord Charles Cornwallis
Picture courtesy of http://commons.wikimedia.org/wiki/
File:Lord_Cornwallis.jpg

Banastre Tarleton
Picture courtesy of http://en.wikipedia.org/wiki/File:Banastre-
Tarleton-by-Joshua-Reynolds.jpg

Daniel Boone
Picture courtesy of http://en.wikipedia.org/wiki/
File:Daniel_Boone.jpg

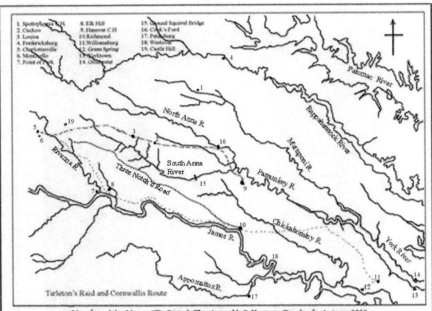

Map from John Maass, "To Disturb The Assembly," *Virginia Cavalcade*, Autumn 2000

Cornwallis' Army Route in Virginia 1781

May 24-27	Petersburg to Westover
May 27-28	Westover to Bottoms Bridge
May 28-29	Bottoms Bridge to New Castle
May 29-31	New Castle, Hanover C.H., Cook's Ford, Ground Squirrel Bridge
June 7-14	Elk Hill
July 4	Depart Williamsburg for Jamestown
	To cross James River in route to Portsmouth
July 6	Battle of Green Spring
Tarleton's Raid	
June 3	Departed Hanover C.H.
June 4	Monticello and Charlottesville
June 7-14	Joined Cornwallis at Elk Hill

Cornwallis intercepts patriot letters

On May 30, 1781, Cornwallis was camped on the North Anna River at Hanover Courthouse north of Richmond. While there, some of his men captured important American dispatches. From them, Cornwallis learned Governor Jefferson and Virginia's General Assembly had left the capital of Richmond. They would regroup in Charlottesville on June 4. He also learned patriot General Friedrich von Steuben was collecting military stores and equipment at Point of Fork located in Goochland County where the Rivanna River flows into the James River.[31]

Cornwallis immediately moved his troops to Cook's Ford on the south side of the North Anna River. That was near where the road from Richmond to Fredericksburg crossed the river. They made camp. From this location on June 3 Cornwallis sent Tarleton to Charlottesville to disrupt the General Assembly and capture Thomas Jefferson.

He also sent Colonel John Graves Simcoe to Point of Fork to destroy patriot war supplies stored there.[32] Virginia War Commissioner Colonel William Davies worried that, "if these stores [at Point of Fork] are lost, the whole wealth of the state in its present situation can never replace them."[33]

This two-pronged British attack was the gravest threat to Virginia since the war began, and to complicate the situation, no one from Governor Jefferson down to the local militia leaders saw the danger until it was almost too late.[34] It was not until May 31 that the Marquis de Lafayette realized Virginia had become the central theater of the war.[35]

Cornwallis followed General John Graves Simcoe and by June 7, he was camped at Jefferson's Elk Hill farm, located some twenty-nine miles southeast of Monticello, on the upper James River.[36]

Tarleton Dispatched

Tarleton was twenty-six years old and had risen quickly through the military ranks because of his fast riding, hard fighting and ruthlessly aggressive nature. Historian Winthrop Sargent said that in English eyes, Tarleton was "a capital horseman, the very model of a partisan (guerrilla) leader."[37]

In his book, *Campaigns of 1780 and 1781 in the Southern Provinces of North America*, Tarleton noted that because of the superiority of their army and the great superiority of the light horse, the British could travel the country without apprehension or difficulty.[38]

Tarleton had 180 Loyalist soldiers. They were Americans from New York, New Jersey, Philadelphia and New York City who fought for the British. These dragoons—riders trained to fight on the ground—were supported by Captain Forbes Champagne of the 23rd Regiment of the Royal Welsh Fusiliers and seventy mounted infantry.[39]

Tarleton and his men left on June 3 and followed the North Anna River on the south bank in Hanover County, then went through Brown's Ordinary in western Hanover County at dawn. They followed the main road leading westward to Ground Squirrel Bridge over the South Anna River. After they were across the river, Tarleton turned west and entered Louisa County on the road to the Louisa Courthouse.[40] The extreme heat obliged Tarleton to stop in the hottest time of the day to rest the men and horses.[41]

Cuckoo Tavern was located on the road before the town of Louisa. Tarleton went by the tavern about thirty minutes before he stopped for the night. He said they rested "at eleven near Louisa County Courthouse and remained at a plenteous plantation till two o'clock in the morning, at which time they resumed their march."[42]

Jack Jouett saw Tarleton

Jouett saw Tarleton's men go by the Cuckoo Tavern on Sunday night June 3 about ten-thirty. He knew who they were and where they were going. He was aware Thomas Jefferson had returned to Monticello after hours of meetings in Charlottesville. Many legislators had remained in town.[43]

Jouett knew he was the only person who could save the Governor. There wasn't time to get help. He had to make his decision and act immediately. The brave Jouett quickly saddled his horse named Sally. They began the forty-mile trip to warn Jefferson and the gentlemen of the General Assembly.

The day had been dark and rainy; however, evening skies cleared and revealed a bright, nearly full moon.[44] Jouett had no way of knowing if he would arrive in time. The possibility of failure surely haunted him.

Jouett assumed Tarleton would stay on the main road to Louisa, then continue to Charlottesville. Jouett had to catch up with, then get around the British and stay south of the enemy. He probably left the Cuckoo area and traveled on the main road for a short time and then went south to distance himself from Tarleton's route. Being familiar with the countryside, he was able to use overgrown, little-used trails, known only to locals.

He later followed a seldom used path called the Old Mountain Road, part of which is now named Jack Jouett Road. As he hurried through the rough paths, Jouett's clothes were torn by low branches, tall bushes and hanging vines. His face was scarred for life.

Tarleton mentioned that the next morning, June 4, twelve American supply wagons and their drivers were captured near Boswell's Tavern. Tarleton took time to burn the wagons and contents. The tavern is located near the intersection of Route 22 and Route 15.[45]

Tarleton's men intercepted a message meant for Dr. Thomas Walker telling him and his guests that the British were coming their way. Of course, with that knowledge, Tarleton had to pay them a visit. He stopped at Dr Walker's home named Castle Hill. Tarleton sent a raiding party to the next estate, named Belvoir, home of Dr. Walker's son, John Walker.[46] Members of the General Assembly were found at both places.

These gentlemen, who had fled from Richmond to the mountains for security, were taken without warning. Some of the men were paroled and left with their families; others, who were suspected to be more hostile in their sentiments, were taken prisoner. As a delaying action, Dinah Walker, wife of Dr. Walker, held the British at Castle Hill longer than they intended by preparing food for them.[47] Tarleton said they didn't stay long.[48]

Jouett crossed the Rivanna River on the outskirts of Charlottesville about three hours before Tarleton's forces. He rode up the mountain and arrived at Monticello about four-thirty in the morning.

Thomas Jefferson was outside with gardener Antonio Giannini[49] when Jouett arrived to warn that the British were coming. Jouett enjoyed a glass or two of Mr. Jefferson's very fine Madeira wine, then he remounted his horse and rode to Charlottesville to warn the General Assembly members staying there.

Jefferson and his guests were far from panic stricken by Jouett's news. They breakfasted at leisure, and later the assemblymen left to join their colleagues in town. Jefferson remained at Monticello and prepared to send his family to safety, including his fragile wife, who was recovering from a difficult delivery and the death of their infant daughter just two months before. His two small daughters and wife were sent to Enniscorthy, the John Coles estate a few miles distant, by way of Blenheim, the Edward Carter estate.[50]

Closer to Charlottesville, at Pen Park, the home of George and Elizabeth Gilmer, a man tried to escape by mounting his horse; he was shot and taken with the British. However, Mrs. Gilmer rushed after the soldiers and implored Tarleton to release her guest. Surprisingly, Tarleton not only released the wounded man but also sent his medical officer back to the home to care for the injured man.[51]

In Charlottesville very early on June 4, Jouett found some legislators sleeping at his father's Swan Tavern and told them to leave because Tarleton was coming. He went door to door in town warning other people of the impending raid.

However, the men could not believe the news. Benjamin Harrison and Archibald Cary, who had come down from Monticello, recalled that some legislators were "so incredulous" Jouett had a hard time getting them to leave. It was only Jack's "extraordinary exertions" that finally made the men believe him.[52]

However, the General Assemblymen met long enough to pass a resolution to abandon Charlottesville and go farther west over the Blue Ridge Mountains to meet in Staunton.[53]

Jouett remained in town

Tarleton arrived outside Charlottesville early on Monday morning June 4. He thought a march of seventy miles in twenty-four hours, with the precautions he had taken, would give him the advantage of surprise. The raid was going so well he pushed his men on to their destination thinking the quicker they arrived the less formidable resistance they would find.[54]

Tarleton's advance dragoons reported back that the Rivanna River's crossing point (Secretary's Ford) was guarded. This is probably where patriot General Charles Scott and the militia were sent. An attack was ordered. The cavalry charged through the water with very few losses. The patriot soldiers who had rushed there were routed.[55]

With his term of office expired, Jefferson was no longer governor of Virginia. He would not go to Staunton. After his guests left, Jefferson began packing documents and spent nearly two hours securing his personal papers and getting ready to leave his home. He also had to hide documents that had state information.[56]

Jefferson had always regretted the loss of his papers in the fire at his home at Shadwell. This time there was not only the danger of loss but also the possibility that information useful to the enemy would fall into their hands.[57]

A Second Warning

A couple of hours after Jouett climbed the mountain to warn Governor Jefferson, another Virginia militiaman was about four miles east of Monticello. Lieutenant Christopher Hudson knew the British were in the area. The twenty-three-year-old neighbor of Jefferson was planning to join Lafayette and his men.

Being near Jefferson's home might have reminded Hudson of seeing then-Governor Jefferson in Richmond in January (1781) preparing for Arnold's invasion.

Hudson met a Mr. Long on the road, and they discussed the movements of the British soldiers in the area. Long said that Jack Jouett had gone to Charlottesville to warn the General Assemblymen of Tarleton's approach, but he didn't know if Jouett had gone to Monticello.[58] Hudson worried that Jefferson might not be aware of the British presence. He turned his horse around and headed toward Monticello. (There is more information about Hudson's statement on page 86.)

Once across the Rivanna River, Tarleton detached Captain Kenneth McLeod and his men to go up the mountain to Monticello and capture Jefferson.[59]

When Lieutenant Hudson arrived, he saw only one person, a gardener. There should have been laborers and craftsmen working in the area. The place was eerily silent and deserted. There certainly was no one to protect Mr. Jefferson.[60]

Hudson entered the house and said he "found Mr. Jefferson perfectly tranquil and undisturbed."[61]

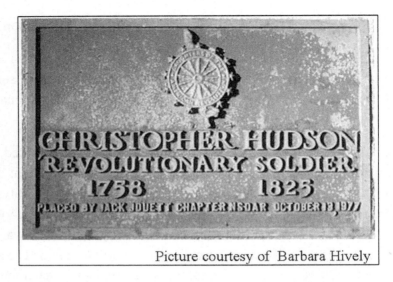

CHRISTOPHER HUDSON
REVOLUTIONARY SOLDIER
1758   1825
PLACED BY JACK JOUETT CHAPTER NSDAR OCTOBER 13, 1977

Picture courtesy of Barbara Hively

Hudson told Jefferson that the British were coming up the hill of Monticello. Jefferson was still not quite ready to leave. Hudson said, "At my earnest request he left his house." It was surrounded in ten minutes [or less] by a troop of light horse.[62]

Jefferson had earlier ordered his favorite horse be taken to a place between Monticello and Carter's Mountain and tied there.[63] After leaving his home, Jefferson walked to a point on the road between Monticello and nearby Carter's Mountain and knelt to set up the tripod for his telescope. He scanned the Charlottesville streets. Not seeing any activity and hearing no approaching hoofbeats on the mountainside, he started walking back to his house for a few last-minute arrangements. On the way to the house, he noticed he had lost his light sword when he knelt to set up his tripod. Jefferson returned to the observation place to pick it up.[64] He focused his telescope for a final look toward the town and was startled to see British dragoons in their green uniforms faced with white, and mounted infantrymen, wearing red coats, swarming in the streets.[65]

Jefferson mounted his favorite horse, a six-year-old stallion named Caractacus, and knowing he would be pursued if he took the road, he "plunged into the woods of the mountain" eluding Tarleton's' men. About five minutes after Jefferson left his home, the British arrived.[66] If Jefferson had gone back to his house after not seeing the redcoats in town (with his spyglass), he would have been captured within minutes.

As for Jefferson, Tarleton reported, "The attempt to secure Mr. Jefferson was ineffectual."[67] According to Tarleton, Mr. Jefferson discovered the British dragoons from his house, on a mountain above the town, before they could approach him. "Jefferson provided for his personal liberty by a precipitate retreat."[68]

At Monticello after Jefferson left, two black men, Martin Hemings, a butler, and Caesar were hiding pieces of silver in a storage area, covered by wooden planks. The area was under a bow of the parlor, which had been added without a full basement. Caesar was down in the storage area receiving the plates when Martin Hemings saw the British arrive. He quickly replaced the planks, covering both the dishes and Caesar.[69]

When one of the British soldiers cocked his gun and put it to Hemings' head, he asked where Mr. Jefferson was. The soldier threatened to shoot if the butler did not answer. Hemings refused to answer and said, "Fire away, then." The redcoat did not shoot. The British remained at Monticello for eighteen hours.[70]

Jefferson joined his family

Later in the day, Jefferson joined his family for dinner at Blenheim,[71] the home of friend Colonel Edward Carter that was seven miles away. However, before evening, Jefferson started on a difficult and tiring trip with his fragile wife and two small daughters. They traveled several days and went ninety miles further to the southwest. When he arrived at another farm he owned, Poplar Forest (in Bedford County outside of Lynchburg), he felt his family was safe and secure.

Meanwhile at Monticello, the enemy searched for Jefferson, but they found some of his finest wine. Perhaps while consuming it they had a toast to King George III, because it was the king's forty-third birthday. The soldiers remained at Monticello until the next day and did not disturb anything on Jefferson's property. This was returning the courtesy with which Jefferson had treated the British and Hessian prisoners from the British defeat at Saratoga in 1777. Those prisoners had been quartered at the Albemarle Barracks near Charlottesville.[72]

MAP Courtesy of Special Collections Library, University of Virginia

Extracted from Pitner's 1920 City of Charlottesville, Virginia

According to the late John Cook Wyllie, Librarian at the University of Virginia, Tarleton entered Charlottesville by way of Belmont approximately along Broadway Street, Carlton Avenue, Monticello Road and up 7th Street to High Street[73] and to Courthouse Square.

Daniel Boone encountered Tarleton

Daniel Boone was one of the last of the Assemblymen in Charlottesville after Jouett had warned the patriots and just before

Tarleton raided the town. Boone was new to the legislature, having been sworn in on May 24.

According to his son, Colonel Nathan Boone, at the time of his capture, Daniel Boone was in Charlottesville and had been securing important papers and public records to protect them from the British. Jouett gave notice of Tarleton's approach. Daniel Boone and others remained loading public records in wagons until troops of the British light horse entered the town.[74] Boone and Jouett started to leave in a slow, unconcerned walk when they were overtaken, questioned hastily, then dismissed. Boone had probably finished being questioned and started to walk away. When Jouett was finished being questioned, he called out to Boone, "Wait a minute, Captain Boone, and I'll go with you."[75]

Upon hearing of his military rank, the redcoats stopped Boone and took him captive.[76] He was kept overnight in the coal cellar at the Nicholas Lewis' plantation located outside of town. He was released the next day.

Tarleton, in his makeshift headquarters at the same plantation, took a nap in what might have been a carriage house while his men roamed Charlottesville.[77]

The house of Nicholas Lewis would be at the present intersection of Twelfth Street Northeast and East Jefferson Street. The western part of the plantation, later called "The Farm" is at 309 Twelfth Street Northeast. It is probably very close to the site of both the main house and the coal house.[78] In 1781, the Lewis Plantation extended to the Rivanna River and later part became Meade Park.[79]

It is interesting that Jack Jouett and Daniel Boone remained in Charlottesville after Jouett's ride was completed and while the British were in town. If Tarleton had known Jouett ruined his mission,

Jouett would have been captured. Jouett was brave to have remained in town, with fresh wounds on his face, after Tarleton's men arrived.

Nathan Boone said[80] years later that his father probably pretended contentment and sung songs while captured. When he was taken to Tarleton the next day, his face and clothes were blackened from the coal dust. Daniel Boone's rank of captain dated back to his commission during the fighting of "Dunmore's War" in 1774, against the Indians on the western frontier before the Revolution.[81]

Much later when Boone finally returned home, he learned he had a son born on the previous March 2. That son was Nathan, who later gave the interview that tells of the above incident.[82]

The British destroyed county records, some arms and other supplies in Charlottesville. They occupied Charlottesville for one day before a violent rainstorm threatened to flood the Rivanna River, prompting Tarleton to ford the rising river and leave town on June 5.

Tarleton must have been in a bad mood after his failure to capture Jefferson. In Goochland County by the James River, on his way to rejoin Cornwallis, he raided "Rock Castle," the home of a distant American cousin, Colonel Tarleton Fleming. On seeing the Tarleton coat of arms displayed in the home of a patriot, Tarleton took the coat of arms plaque with him and set fire to the house. The fire was quickly extinguished and very little damage occurred.[83]

Also on June 5, British Colonel Simcoe's men captured and destroyed some American supplies at Point of Fork, which was Steuben's main supply point. Steuben and his men had managed to remove and hide some of the supplies.

Old Court House Square, Charlottesville, Virginia

Historic Court Square

This building, in continuous use as a courthouse for over 200 years, is one of America's most historic. No other courthouse has been used by three early American Presidents at the same time. The original wood frame courthouse was erected on a two-acre lot in 1762 when the city was founded by Dr. Thomas Walker. Here local elections were held and the County Court conducted business with the help of young attorneys and magistrates such as Thomas Jefferson and James Monroe. These men along with

James Madison later became Presidents and could at times be seen here together.

After a stirring patriotic sermon by Rev. Charles Clay on a public Fast Day in 1774 the freeholders of Albemarle County met here and made a resolution to the Virginia House of Burgesses that called for a boycott of trade with England and for a meeting of a Continental Congress. When the British attacked Richmond in the summer of 1781 the Virginia General Assembly made Charlottesville its temporary emergency capital and met here for deliberations, including Patrick Henry, Benjamin Harrison, Thomas Nelson, Richard Henry Lee, John Tyler and Daniel Boone.

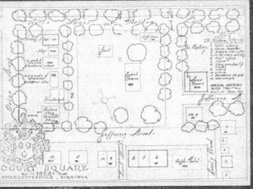

The courthouse was also a place of worship and Jefferson himself helped organize an independent congregation led by Rev. Clay beginning in 1777 called the Calvinistical Reformed Church. A member of this church, Col John Harvie, introduced Jefferson's famous Bill for Religious Freedom to the Virginia legislature that same year. Many years later Jefferson called the courthouse the "common temple" and proudly spoke of its use each Sunday by four Protestant denominations in turn.

The square was enclosed with a railing in 1792 and a second building of brick was built in place of the wooden structure in 1803 and now forms the north wing to your right. It faced a public square with taverns and shops behind you (on today's Park Street). A whipping post, stocks, pillory and a stone jail stood on this public square that also was the commercial center of the town. The south wing of this courthouse, which is located behind this display was built in 1860 in the Gothic Revival style and was modified to its current appearance in the 1930's as part of an extensive renovation. This work restored the Colonial features of the original building and remodeled the portico in the Colonial Revival style.

Results of Jack Jouett's Ride

Jack Jouett's ride saved from capture the following men:

<u>Thomas Jefferson</u>, the author of the Declaration of Independence. He was considered a traitor by the British. Until June 2, 1781, he was Governor of Virginia. Jefferson sent his family away after Jouett's warning, but he required a second warning from Lieutenant Christopher Hudson to convince him to leave Monticello.

It is impossible to list his many contributions to our American lives. Some of the most important are: he was the Vice President under John Adams; he became the third president of the United States; he increased the size of the United States when he bought the Louisiana Territory in 1803; and he was the founder of the University of Virginia.

<u>Archibald Cary</u> served in the Colonial House of Burgesses beginning in 1756. He was a member when Royal Governor Dunmore dissolved the House of Burgesses in 1774, because of its resolutions censuring and condemning the closing of Boston's port by the British. Cary then served as a delegate to the Virginia Conventions, and he was chairman of the committee that instructed the Virginia Delegates to declare independence from the Mother Country at the Second Continental Congress. He gave funds to underwrite the cost of the Virginia militia because of British attempts to promote the sale of slaves in the American colonies. This was after slavery was abolished in England. At the time of Tarleton's raid, Cary was the Speaker of the Senate of Virginia. He kept that position until his death in 1787. He escaped capture at Monticello.[84]

Benjamin Harrison was elected to the Colonial House of Burgesses at the age of 38. In 1764, when the House defied the Royal Governor and passed the Stamp Act Resolutions, the Royal Governor tried to bribe Harrison with an appointment to the Executive Council (the governor's cabinet). Harrison declined the offer. Later at the Second Continental Congress on July 1, 1776, Congress agreed that the Declaration of Independence be considered by Harrison's Committee of the Whole. Having further amended the Declaration on July 2 and 3, his Committee adopted the document in its final form on Thursday, July 4. Harrison duly reported this action to the Congress and delivered to the Congress a final reading of the Declaration of Independence.[85]

Harrison was chosen Speaker of the Virginia House of Delegates in 1778, and was Speaker when he escaped capture at Monticello. He was elected Governor of the State of Virginia in 1782. He retired from the Governor's office after five years of service. His son, William Henry Harrison, was the ninth United States President, and his great-grandson, Benjamin Harrison, was the twenty-fourth President of the United States. Harrison County in West Virginia (formed in 1784) is named after Benjamin Harrison.[86]

Richard Henry Lee wrote the Westmoreland Resolution to oppose the Stamp Act. The Resolution was publicly signed by more than one hundred prominent landowners at Leedstown, Westmoreland County, on February 27, 1766. Several brothers of George Washington also signed the Resolution. Lee worked on the House of Burgesses committee that drafted a letter to King George III warning him not to impose direct taxes on Virginia (1774). He created the Committees of Correspondence among the many independent-minded American men in the thirteen colonies leading up to the Revolution. Lee's resolutions in the Second Continental Congress (1776) led to the colonies declaring their independence.[87]

He was a member of the Virginia House of Delegates, and after the war, a United States Senator who became the President pro tempore (temporary leader) during his term in the Congress.

In June 1787, in the Congress, he helped draft the Northwest Ordinance establishing the Northwest Territory of Ohio, Indiana, Illinois, Wisconsin, Michigan and Minnesota. When the new Constitution was being proposed, Lee saw its strengths over the old Articles of Confederation and suggested several amendments and a bill of rights like George Mason's Declaration of Rights to the Virginia Constitution. A bitterness that developed during the public debates over the document shortened Lee's role in the ratification debates. He escaped capture at Monticello.[88]

Brigadier General Thomas Nelson, Jr., was a member of the House of Burgesses in 1774, when it was dissolved by Royal Governor Dunmore. The Royal Governor was angry because the Burgesses resolutions censured and condemned the closing of the Port of Boston by the British. To protest this action, Nelson began spending some of his personal fortune, sending needed supplies to Boston. He was one of the men who organized a Yorktown Tea Party on the morning of November 7, 1774. Nelson threw two half-chests of tea from the brig *Virginia* into the York River. Nelson urged armed resistance to Great Britain as early as 1775.[89]

In May 1777, Nelson suffered the first of many strokes. He seemed to recover, but continued to have additional strokes as well as periodic bouts of asthma. Despite these health problems, he remained active in politics. In 1781, he was elected Governor of Virginia, succeeding Jefferson. However, he was not able to serve his full term. To the British, he was an enemy officer and one of the men who helped finance the war in Virginia.

The Virginia State Council for Higher Education named Thomas Nelson Community College located on the Virginia Peninsula in Nelson's honor in 1967. Nelson County, Virginia and Nelson County, Kentucky are both named in his honor.[90]

Patrick Henry was, in 1765, elected to the House of Burgesses from Louisa County. He introduced the Virginia Stamp Act Resolutions that were possibly the most anti-British American political action to that date. Some credit the Resolutions with being one of the main catalysts of the Revolution. Henry continued his war of words and was called a firebrand of the time. He had been targeted by the British for his leadership in the Revolution. Henry served as a delegate to the Continental Congress from 1775 to 1777 and again in 1779. He was one of the first to favor separation from Britain and urged his fellow delegates to support the cause of independence. He was a strong leader in the General Assembly after it moved to Staunton. He served as the first and sixth post-colonial governors of Virginia.[91]

In 1784, Henry was again elected the Governor of Virginia and served until 1786. He declined to attend the Constitutional Convention because he was against a strong federal government. Henry was instrumental in getting the Bill of Rights adopted to amend the new Constitution to protect individual rights. He did not accept the offer of President George Washington in 1795 to serve as the Secretary of State. Henry later changed his mind about the strong federal government. He was against the Virginia and Kentucky resolutions that would allow a state to nullify a federal law it considered unconstitutional. President John Adams nominated Henry as special emissary to France in 1798, but Henry declined due to failing health.[92]

Counties in eight states are named for him as well as a U.S. army base in Germany. He helped establish Hampden-Sidney College where six of his sons graduated. In Virginia: Emory and Henry College in Emory, Patrick Henry Community College in Martinsville and Patrick Henry College in Purcellville are named for him. At least three U.S. Navy ships and a World War I Army base in Newport News were named after him. The army base became Patrick Henry Airport. Today it is the Newport News/Williamsburg International Airport. There is a Fort Patrick Henry Dam in Tennessee named for him.[93]

Ambrose Rucker was an Assemblyman from Orange County who had served as a captain in the French and Indian War. He moved to Amherst County and was commissioned as a lieutenant colonel in the militia in November 1766. He was reported to be six feet, six inches tall and three hundred pounds in weight. Somehow he managed to get his powerful horse to jump a fence and carry him to safety just as the British were approaching the house where he was spending the night.[94]

General Edward Stevens was an officer and a legislator serving in the Virginia Senate. He was thirty years old when he distinguished himself as a leader at the Battle of Great Bridge (December 9, 1775). He fought in the Battles of Brandywine, Germantown and Camden. He was wounded in the thigh at the Battle of Guilford Courthouse. Stevens was staying at the Swan Tavern in Charlottesville on that fateful night of June 3.

Stevens was recuperating from the wound, so he had a limp. By being shabbily dressed and riding slowly on an old horse, Stevens escaped from Charlottesville. The British probably assumed he was a farmer.[95] Stevens returned to lead men at the Battle of Yorktown.[96]

Jack Jouett: Revolutionary Rider

British Colonel Tarleton was also wounded at The Battle of Guilford Courthouse. He had two fingers shot off his right hand by a rifleman.[97] He was probably learning to conduct war left-handed.

John Tyler, Sr., served in the Continental Army in 1775 and was in the House of Delegates for several years, later becoming the Speaker of the House from 1781 until 1784. After the Revolution, he was the Vice President of the Virginia Convention to ratify the United States Constitution. He was appointed a judge in the Virginia High Court of Admiralty and was consequently a judge on the first Virginia Court of Appeals.

Tyler was Virginia's fifteenth governor. In 1811, he was nominated by President James Madison to the United States District Court for the District of Virginia. Tyler held that position until his death. He was the father of John Tyler, Jr., the tenth President of the United States. Tyler County, West Virginia is named after him.[98]

Some of the men captured by Tarleton

Dr. Thomas Walker was a well-known explorer and physician of Albemarle County. He lived at Castle Hill and had guests who were taken.

Judge Peter Lyons was a lawyer from King William County. He was elected to the General Court which made him an ex-officio member of the Court of Appeals. Lyons was elected by a joint ballot of both Houses of the Assembly. He became President of the Virginia Court of Appeals. A physically very large man, Lyons was captured at Castle Hill but was not taken away as a prisoner.

34

<u>Colonel John Syme</u> was a half-brother of Patrick Henry and a House of Delegates member from Hanover County. He was taken at Dr. Walker's house with Newman Brockenbrough.[99]

Latitude 38.077259 – Longitude 78.29229

<u>Newman Brockenbrough</u>, member of the Virginia House of Delegates endured the difficult ride into captivity.[100]

<u>John Walker</u>, son of Dr. Walker, lived next to his father at his own plantation named Belvoir. John succeeded his father as a Burgess from Albemarle County in 1773. During the early years of the Revolution, John served as an aide to General George Washington.[101]

In 1780, while John Walker was a delegate to the Continental Congress, his only child, Mildred, age fifteen, fell in love with and married Francis Kinloch, a delegate to the Continental Congress from South Carolina. They were married on February 22, 1781, at John Walker's home. The young couple was at Belvoir when Tarleton's dragoons raided and captured both Walker and Kinloch.[102]

The above Francis Kinloch must have felt quite unlucky because he had been captured at the surrender of Charleston in May 1780 and was paroled.[103] This time, he was found hiding at John Walker's home by his cousin, Captain David Kinloch, one of Tarleton's soldiers.[104]

<u>William and Robert Nelson</u>, brothers of Brigadier General Thomas Nelson, Jr., were captured at Belvoir, home of John Walker.

Colonel William Nelson was present at the battles of Monmouth, Brandywine and all the Northern battles in which Washington's army was engaged. He was present at the siege of Yorktown in 1781.

<u>James Lyons,</u> son of Judge Peter Lyons,[105] and <u>Captain John Syme</u> son of Colonel John Syme were taken.

<u>James Hayes</u> had been captured by Tarleton three years earlier. Governor Jefferson had selected him with John Dunlop, a Philadelphia printer, to establish a press in Richmond. They were to print for the Commonwealth and issue a newspaper. One press was captured by the British in transit from Philadelphia. Hayes set up another press in Richmond during April 1781. Almost immediately,

he moved it to Charlottesville when that village became the seat of government. Shortly after his capture, Hayes was released by Cornwallis and made his way to Staunton where the legislature had reassembled. Hayes returned to Richmond and published his first issue of *The Virginia Gazette, or, The American Advertiser* on December 22, 1781.[106] Hayes was the state printer whose job it was to print state currency.[107]

Dudley Diggs, the President of the Executive Council and former lieutenant governor of Virginia was captured.[108] The Diggs family had participated in colonial government since 1650. This event ended his political involvement in the American Revolution. He did remain active in Virginia government and helped to write the state's first constitution.[109]

Brigadier General Charles Scott, who had fought at the Battle of Great Bridge, was captured at Charleston, South Carolina in 1780 and paroled there. He was captured again in Charlottesville. He later became a Governor of Kentucky[110]

Thomas Swearingen, a delegate from Fayette County (in the western part of Virginia that is now Kentucky) was captured. He only attended six days of the Assembly during the Session and most likely went home after his release.[111]

Daniel Boone, who also represented Fayette County, was taken in Charlottesville.[112]

Most of the men were taken to Elk Hill, Jefferson's plantation that Cornwallis was using as his headquarters. Tarleton retained those of the lower class, lacking wealth or position, as prisoners of war. Two weeks later Patrick Henry received a letter from a man in Pennsylvania concerning James Rice, one of the "Pennsylvania Waggoners" who, with two others, were "taken by Colonel

Tarleton."[113] They must have been with the twelve wagons Tarleton captured at daybreak near Boswell's Tavern.

British incursions on the James River included the destruction of the important Chickahominy Shipyard on the Chickahominy River at Shipyard Creek. A complete victory was accomplished over the Virginia Navy at Osborne's Landing at the mouth of the Appomattox River.

British Destruction

There were three basic reasons the British were able to travel around the state and destroy at will.

1. The British had complete control of the rivers, including the James, Potomac, York and Rappahannock as well as many smaller rivers like the Chickahominy and Appomattox. They could move soldiers faster by taking men and their horses on boats and moving them up and down the rivers.[114]

British raids on the James River in April had almost destroyed the Virginia Navy. A shipyard on the Chickahominy River, located off the James River, was destroyed on April 18. A complete victory occurred at Osborne's Landing located near the entrance of the Appomattox River on April 27. The ships were undermanned and had insufficient guns and ammunition to fight off the British. The redcoats burned or captured merchant ships and nine smaller boats of the Virginia Navy. A boat named the *Jefferson* was also lost. Twelve private ships holding two thousand hogshead of tobacco were captured.[115]

2. Cornwallis's army, numbering about 7,000 men, was better trained, better equipped and larger than any militia units of the state.[116]

3. The British had five hundred mounted infantry and could cover territory much faster than the few American militia units. The enemy was constantly stealing patriot horses as fast as they could find them. The patriot militia had only sixty cavalry horses. Legislators, who had considerable wealth in fine horses, were well aware their policy against militia horse impressments was hurting Lafayette. There were laws to keep the militia from impressing horses. However, the

wealthy plantation owners still lost their finest horses, stolen by the British. These horses became an advantage for the British as they constantly added mounted troops to their army.[117]

There were still enough loyalists living in Virginia to help lead British soldiers to hidden American stores. The British were good at intimidating citizens as they took their food and livestock.

When considering the amount of destruction the British were able to inflict, it should be remembered that when Charleston, South Carolina fell to the British on May 12, 1780, the entire southern army was taken. Charleston's surrender was the worst loss of the entire war for the American Colonies. Over five thousand American men and officers were captured. There was a tremendous loss of materiel: 309 artillery pieces, nearly six thousand muskets, 3,300 rounds of ammunition and three frigates were among the lost materiel.[118]

For the Americans, many officers were paroled; however, it was a tremendous loss because most of the soldiers taken as prisoners were not released until after the war, if they could live that long in captivity on the British prison ships.[119] Many other Virginia soldiers were with General Greene fighting in the more southern states.

Damage on the James and Potomac Rivers

On the James River, the new capital of Richmond and the town of Petersburg[120] had been raided; tobacco, homes, a gun foundry (in Richmond) and civic records had been burned or otherwise destroyed.

Much of the damage done by the British in 1781 was along the James River. However, the Potomac River was hit extremely hard by Captain Thomas Graves and ships under his command. He was a cousin of Admiral Lord Thomas Graves, who had been commander-in-chief of British naval forces in North America. Captain Graves had arrived in Virginia waters with Admiral Marriot Arbuthnot's fleet on March 4, 1781.[121]

Captain Graves left Hampton on April 3, in his sloop HMS *Savage,* leading a small flotilla of escort vessels that included the HMS *Swift,* HMS *Rambler,* sloops HMS *General Monk* and HMS *Hope.* On the Potomac River, they managed to destroy vast amounts of tobacco, the money crop of the colonies.[122] They successfully damaged or destroyed private property along both the Virginia and Maryland shores of the river.

British landing parties began their raids by offering to purchase food and other supplies. When the patriots refused to sell to the enemy, the British would take what they wanted by force and destroy everything they couldn't take with them.

The looting and destroying of plantations resulted in many homes being burned to the ground. Trails of destruction were evident as smoke rose above the burning homes. Winds on the river lifted smoke to the sky, warning neighbors of the coming evil. Also lost were tobacco warehouses, crops and small manufacturing establishments. The raiders made examples of the uncooperative homeowners who suffered much worse damage than those who cooperated.

When Mount Vernon, General Washington's home was threatened, a cousin left in charge of the home gave into British demands and provided food for the enemy. This was against the General's instructions and wishes. Washington was angry when he learned what had happened. He had been more worried the British would kidnap his wife Martha and hold her hostage than he was about his beloved home. She was not at Mount Vernon when this raid occurred. Because of the shifting mud banks in the Potomac River, the enemy did not get up river far enough to destroy the city of Alexandria.

Captain Graves summed up his experiences on the Potomac River by reporting, with cold finality, "Burnt all their Houses."[123]

Elsewhere in the state

There was practically no organized resistance in the state and no military force of consequence to oppose the British. They moved at will around the Tidewater region of the state. Governor Thomas Jefferson's administration seemed helpless and impotent in the face of British aggression.[124]

In June on their way to Charlottesville the British stopped in Hanover County at the home of Ann Nicholas, widow of Robert Carter Nicholas, former colonial treasurer. The large British army, camp followers and freed blacks seized crops, cattle, hogs, sheep and chickens for their meals and cooked the meat over fires that burned fences and outbuildings they had torn down.[125]

Even though it was not safe, a few days after the British raid on his home in June, Jefferson returned to Monticello to see if had been destroyed. While high in the mountains, he had an extraordinary view of the James River. He could see the devastation being wrought by the British along the James River as smoke from the burning houses and property successively rose on the horizon at a distance for twenty-five or thirty miles.[126]

Military supplies destroyed

The redcoats had ransacked Charlottesville, destroyed one thousand muskets, four hundred barrels of gunpowder, clothing, tobacco and county records. By this time, all but twenty British soldiers from the Albemarle Barracks outside of Charlottesville had been moved to Maryland. These twenty soldiers from the Battle of Saratoga joined Tarleton's men.

At Point of Fork, British Colonel Simcoe destroyed 2,500 stands of arms, 150 barrels of gun powder and shot, a 13-inch mortar, five brass howitzers, four brass cannon, a large quantity of saltpeter and sulfur needed for making gun powder, brandy and a great variety of small items necessary for equipping cavalry and infantry.[127]

Elk Hill laid waste

Elk Hill farm was property inherited from Jefferson's wife's family. He knew it would be a prime target of the British and had gone there in early May to removed most of the things he considered valuable. Many of his horses were left behind.

After Cornwallis and his seven thousand soldiers spent ten days camping in the corn and tobacco fields of Elk Hill, there could not have been much left to harvest. In addition to the soldiers, there were hundreds of camp followers that included wives and children who needed to be fed. Captain Johann Ewald, a Hessian, estimated that four thousand freed slaves travelled with the soldiers for whom they worked. Wherever Cornwallis camped with his soldiers, camp followers and slaves, that location became the largest city in Virginia.[128]

Cornwallis's army wrought devastation at Elk Hill far and wide. Not content with burning the barns that contained crops harvested during the prior year, they tore down and burned fences and outbuildings. They took the horses and cattle and cut the throats of the colts too young to be useful. Cornwallis carried off thirty black people. Jefferson said that if Cornwallis was going to free the slaves, he thought that was good. However, Cornwallis was not kind to them and housed them with other slaves who were suffering from small pox and "putrid fever," (typhus) and most of them died.[129]

The British soldiers raided other homes in the Elk Hill area for food and plunder.[130] However, Elk Hill suffered the worst. Jefferson did not quarrel with Cornwallis's right to feed his men with the spoils of war. He was angry that Cornwallis had allowed his troops to ruin and burn nearly everything.[131] During this time some legislators discussed whether negotiations with the British would be necessary to end the war.[132]

History repeats itself in a church

Amid the British destruction and the rampage of Cornwallis and Tarleton's troops, it was time for the General Assembly to meet. The Revolution in Virginia was at its lowest point. The General Assembly members were afraid to meet in Richmond. They might have remembered how in 1774, Lord Dunmore had dissolved their House of Burgesses. The men had moved to nearby Raleigh Tavern, renamed themselves the Virginia Convention and continued to meet. In 1775, they met in Richmond to get away from Dunmore and his Royal Marines. They used the Henrico Parish Church[133] because it was the only building large enough to hold all of them. It was there Patrick Henry gave his firebrand speech asking for "liberty or death" that ignited their spirits and pushed them toward their pursuit of Independence. The church was renamed St. John's Church.

Assembly Moved to Staunton

In June 1781 the General Assembly was again on the run. This time they went from Richmond to Charlottesville, then over the Blue Ridge mountains to Stanton.

This plaque located at Trinity church commemorates the meeting of the Virginia Assembly June 7–23, 1781. It lists the Assembly members who met in the Old Parish Church building.

It was erected by the Beverley Manor Chapter, Daughters of the American Revolution, June 7, 1913.

Picture courtesy of Gary Persinger

Twenty-one Senators and sixty-one members of the House of Delegates arrived in Staunton and again found protection in a church for their meeting house. The old Augusta Parish Church stood about where the tower is located on Trinity Episcopal Church at 214 West Beverley Street, Staunton. For this General Assembly Session the church served as the Virginia State Capitol.[134]

The names listed below are on the plaque located outside of Trinity Episcopal Church. These determined men in their persistence and diligence fulfilled their responsibilities to their state and country.

Senators who met in Staunton, June 7–23, 1781

Richard Adams	William Fleming
Isaac Avery	Corbin Griffin
Burwell Bassett	Nathaniel Harrison
William Cabell	Thomas Jett
Archibald Cary	John Jones
Aug. Claiborne	Henry Lee
Walter Coles	Paul Loyall
Thomas Elliot	Sampson Matthews
William Ellsey	Robert Rutherford
Edward Stevens	Edmond Winston
James Taylor	

Delegates who met in Staunton, June 7–23, 1781

Richard Baker	Andrew Moore
Henry Bell	Haynes Morgan
Abraham Bird	Thomas Mountjoy
Daniel Boone	James Neal
John Bowdoin	George Nicholas
John Breckenridge	Mann Page
Lewis Burwell	Charles Patteson
William Cabell	Francis Peyton
Charles Campbell	William Pickett
William Campbell	John Powell
Robert Clark	William Royall
George Clendenin	Ambrose Rucker
Robert Craves	Peter Saunders
Cole Diggs	Johnny Scott
John Edwards	Thomas Smith
Henry Fields	Turner Southall
Thomas Flournoy	James Steel
James Garrard	French Strother
William Green	John Talbot
Benjamin Harrison	John Taylor
Patrick Henry	Champion Travis

Nicholas Hobson
James Innes
Zachariah Johnson
Benjamin Lankford
Aaron Lewis
Samuel Lewis
Benjamin Logan
Thomas Lomax
William Mayo
Daniel McCarty

Sylvanus Walker
Michael Wallace
George Watkins
Joel Watkins
William White
Benjamin Wilson
Beverly Winslow
John Woodson
Edward Young

When the Virginia General Assembly arrived in Staunton they had no clear leader. Thomas Jefferson was out of office and did not attend the Session. The House of Delegates had reduced the number of members needed for a quorum to forty when it met in Charlottesville. However the upper house, the Senate, had not reduced their number needed to establish a quorum so they were delayed in getting started.

The president of the Executive Council should have acted as executive of the Staunton Session. However, Dudley Diggs had resigned when Jefferson moved the government to Charlottesville. The Executive Council never had a quorum to elect his replacement. The next person in line was David Jameson who was in Richmond. He didn't go to Charlottesville until July. The third in line was Dr. William Fleming. He had not attended a Session since April.[135]

In order to avoid a situation like this, Jefferson had asked Dr. William Fleming and Andrew Lewis to be certain to attend the meetings in Staunton. Dr. Fleming arrived on June 13, 1781, and was the only representative of the Executive Council in Stanton. He therefore led the meetings without becoming acting governor. The assemblymen referred to Dr. Fleming as a member of the Privy Council. He, like Jefferson, doubted he had the authority to call out the militia.[136]

Dr. Fleming had to protect the state and conduct its business. After Thomas Nelson, Jr. was elected governor the General Assembly authorized Dr. Fleming's actions while in office. That made him a legitimate Governor of Virginia.

The House quickly decided they would select a governor on the fifth day of the new session. This was probably to give the Senate members time to get to Staunton and time to meet.

On Sunday, June 10, in the Augusta Parish Church, the House of Delegates provided for another flight. If the redcoats presented themselves in Staunton, the House was to adjourn and meet at Warm Springs, now in West Virginia.

George Webb was the only man to make the trip from Richmond to Charlottesville and to be there on May 24, the day the General Assembly was to meet. He arrived in Staunton on June 12, when William Cabell, Samuel Hardy and Samuel McDowell were elected to the Council of the State. The next day, James Madison, Edmond Randolph, Joseph Jones, Theodorick Bland and John Blair were appointed delegates to the Continental Congress.[137]

Amid the chaos, many Virginians saw their state leadership as dysfunctional and demoralized. George Nicholas, one of the new younger representatives, moved that the General Assembly appoint "…a Dictator…in this Commonwealth who should have the power of disposing of the lives and fortunes of the Citizens thereof without being subject to account."[138] Nicholas suggested either General George Washington or General Nathaniel Green be chosen. Patrick Henry supported the motion and tried to push the measure. The idea of an all-powerful leader began to spread. Richard Henry Lee urged the Congress in Philadelphia to send General Washington back to Virginia as a dictator. Jefferson later said the motion lost by six votes.[139]

General Thomas Nelson was with Lafayette and the army, when elected Governor. He did not reach Staunton to be sworn in until the evening of June 18. Finally after 16 days, Virginia had a new leader.

After meeting in Staunton, Governor Nelson decided to move the executive office back to Charlottesville. He started toward Charlottesville on June 27 and became ill. When he was well and able to work, the Governor and Council met twice while in Charlottesville.[140]

Governor Nelson struggled with governmental responsibilities in the war-weary state. On July 3, the General Assembly left Charlottesville to return to Richmond and was scheduled to meet there on July 9. However, Nelson did not arrive for another two weeks. He did not keep in contact with the War Office.[141] Commissioner of War William Davies wrote to General Steuben on July 12, 1781, saying that for the preceding two weeks no one knew where the new governor was. Nor had anyone gotten any word from him. Davies said in his letter that, "I think we shall be swept off one of these days, I see nothing in the world to prevent it."[142]

Picture courtesy of Gary Persinger

This Windsor chair located in Trinity
Church was used during the meetings
of the General Assembly while in
session in Staunton, June 7-23, 1781.
Chair gift of Harouf Family.

Actions of the Virginia Assembly

The Virginia Assembly was established on July 30, 1619, by representatives of the King of England. The colony had been governed by representatives of the King for one hundred and fifty-seven years.

In 1776, Virginia and the other colonies declared themselves free from of the rule of King George III. The new Virginia constitution included a Bill of Rights. The 1776 leaders were afraid of any strong government that might oppress the people's rights. This handicapped Governor Thomas Jefferson when the British invaded the state.

After the earlier legislature had balked at Jefferson's request for more power to compel militia turnout, the 1781 Staunton session went past those requests and gave General Thomas Nelson, Jr., the new governor, stronger support. These new powers allowed the governor to call out the militia and authorized him to confiscate property of those who opposed the call to duty.[143]

The militia was improved by a number of new regulations which included: equal pay with the continental soldiers and terms of service changed to two months instead of three. In an effort to avoid the new penalties, many deserters returned to duty and pleaded their cases. With the fear of double duty (being called up for continental and militia service) many men found if they joined the militia they were spared continental service. Men preferred to serve within their own state.[144]

With these new rulings, Virginia's Assembly and Governor Thomas Nelson, Jr. were able to lead the state from its lowest point and to continue the fight for survival. Virginia today has the oldest continuous legislative body in the Western Hemisphere.

The Virginia Assembly first met on July 30, 1619

It is the Oldest Legislative Body in the Western Hemisphere.

The Colonial Assembly began with two houses or bodies:

Lower House	Upper House
House of Burgesses	Governor's Council
Each Burgess elected by landowners	12 members selected by the Royal Governor

Royal Governor was sent over from England –ruled over both houses.

The Assembly met in Jamestown from 1619 until 1699.

It then moved to Williamsburg and met in the colonial

Capital Building.

Made laws for the colony	Reviewed laws made by Burgesses. Revised, Approved or Disapproved

The approval of the Burgesses, the Council and the Governor was needed to pass a law.

1776

American Colonies declare independence

Virginia first to write a state constitution

NEW COUNTRY ESTABLISHED

New Virginia Legislature

Lower House becomes House of Delegates	Upper House becomes the Senate

Virginia State Capitol Building
Designed by Thomas Jefferson, cornerstone laid
by Governor Patrick Henry in 1785
Picture from Google public domain

Thomas Jefferson

Picture from Google Public Domain

Monticello   Picture from Google public domain

Conclusion of fighting in Virginia

British forces under Cornwallis had destroyed most of Virginia's war materiel and tobacco, put the governor and legislature to flight and spread fear across the state.[145] After these coordinated and successful attacks, Virginia was reeling from the devastation inflected. The Americans were definitely losing the War for Independence.

Cornwallis believed his primary mission to destroy the military supply system in Virginia had been completed. With fall coming, he began looking for a deep-water port to pass the winter, resupply his men and await his next orders from Clinton in New York City.[146]

Cornwallis received a letter dated June 11 from his commander ordering him to return close to 3,000 of his Virginia troops to New York. Clinton had decided to quit the southern theater and pull his forces back to New York City.[147]

This order must have been disheartening to Cornwallis in knowing how close the British were to victory at that point. However, he felt his had no choice but to comply and thus quit the war in the southern provinces as he had been fighting it.

Captain Johann Ewald, a Hessian officer in Cornwallis' army, wrote in his journal on July 4, "I learned that Lord Cornwallis would march back to the works at Portsmouth, and that the army must go on the defensive."[148]

General Clinton had asked for the 43rd and 76th Regiments for his reinforcement in New York.[149]

A few days later, Cornwallis told Clinton that if he returned the troops, he could not establish a base at Yorktown. He would not have enough men to occupy Gloucester Point across the York River to protect ships moored at Yorktown.

Clinton was described as torn by indecision, "very unfit for his Station" and "very changeable."[150] He finally let Cornwallis decide what he wanted to do. Cornwallis chose to keep all of the soldiers, fortify Yorktown and spend the winter in Virginia.[151]

On June 25, the British reached Williamsburg.[152] Before crossing the James River, Cornwallis set a trap at Green Spring for the patriots who had been following him. They sent the baggage across the river and made the American forces think most of the army had crossed. The Americans believed only a rear guard was at Green Spring. When the patriots attacked the rear guard, it retreated into the woods only to reveal Cornwallis' main body of soldiers. The Americans suffered approximately 200 men killed or wounded at the Battle of Green Spring.

Cornwallis and his army quit the field and moved to Portsmouth where they boarded ships to Yorktown. His army of 1,500 soldiers arrived at Yorktown on August 1. The bulk of his army arrived soon after that date.[153] He asked to be resupplied. Clinton was slow to answer.

Clinton was still worried that Washington would attack his position in New York City. Captain Ewald wrote in his journal that the demonstrations of the American and French armies under Washington and Comte de Rochambeau, which had united at White Plains (New York), were the cause of this swift change from the offensive to the defensive.[154]

In late August, Lafayette secretly asked Governor Nelson to estimate how long Virginia could support twelve thousand troops. They did not want the word to get out that a siege of Cornwallis and his army at Yorktown was possible.[155] Later Lafayette told Nelson about the plans and urged him to prepare Virginia to give every "possible aid and assistance, particularly in respect to supplies."[156] Nelson was overjoyed and set about making plans to prepare for the event. Nelson had great organizational skills that were needed to coordinate the incoming French and American armies. He ordered the counties to send militia to protect the state.[157]

For a while Nelson tried to balance the state business and the war responsibilities. However, he announced that he would take personal command of feeding and housing the Virginia army. He said he would leave state business in the hands of David Jameson. Nelson felt the administration of the war and taking care of military business was more important. In order to have food, weapons and supplies ready for the twelve thousand incoming soldiers, Nelson himself must handle the situation. He realized the patriots might not get another chance to bring the war to a sudden end.

Before Nelson could take care of all the details, he became ill (he had asthma attacks). Lieutenant Governor David Jameson and William Davies in the War Department were extremely able men and they carried through with the plans made before Nelson's illness for gathering supplies and calling the militia. Nelson recovered and was well enough to continue with the details of getting ready for the largest event of the war.[158]

Washington and Rochambeau quietly started marching south before Clinton realized they had left the New York area. Cornwallis did not receive help and was forced to surrender when the French fleet sealed the Chesapeake Bay, including the York and James Rivers.

After Jouett's ride, the war in Virginia lasted four and a half months. Major fighting in the south ended with the surprise surrender of Cornwallis at Yorktown on October 19, 1781.

Thomas Nelson, Jr.
Picture courtesy of Google public domain pictures

Four and a half months after Jack Jouett's ride
Cornwallis surrendered at Yorktown
Oil painting by John Trumbull circa 1819-1820
Public domain picture from http://en.wikipedia.org/wiki/Surrender_of_Lord_Cornwallis

The guns at Yorktown fell silent
Public domain picture of Yorktown battlefield

https://www.google.com/search?
q=public+domain+pictures+of+Yorktown

Jack Jouett after the Ride

The General Assembly quickly honored Jack Jouett (June 15) at their meeting in Old Trinity Church.[159] They adopted the following resolution: "Resolved that the executive be desired to present to Captain John Jouett, Jr. an elegant sword and pair of pistols as a memorial of the high sense which the General Assembly entertain of his activity and enterprise in watching the motions of the enemy's cavalry on their late incursion to Charlottesville and conveying to the assembly timely information of their approach, whereby their designs of the enemy were frustrated and many valuable stores preserved."[160] The pistols were bought from Thomas M. Randolph for eight pounds, ten shillings and given to Jouett in 1783.[161]

A year after he made his important ride, Jack Jouett left Louisa County and moved westward to Mercer County where he served as a Virginia state legislator.[162] He married Sallie Robards Harris on August 20, 1784. She was known for her beauty and social tact.[163] They had twelve children.

Jack was elected as one of the first delegates to the Virginia Legislature from the Kentucky territory in 1787. He was elected to the Virginia Legislature from Mercer County in 1790. Jouett became an active citizen working for Virginia's western land to become a separate state. As a result of his work, on June 1, 1792, Kentucky became our fifteenth state. He represented the same Mercer County in the Kentucky Legislature in 1792.

The Jouett family moved to Woodford County, in the middle of today's Bluegrass Region, in 1795. He was elected to the legislature representing Woodford County from 1795-1796 and 1797.[164] As early as 1787, Jouett was an active and influential member of the Kentucky Society, organized for the promotion of useful knowledge.

From this society grew the organization for the importation of improved breeds of cattle from England. Jouett became a successful planter as well as a breeder of imported cattle and horses.

In Woodford County, he built a fine brick home in or about 1797. The five-room home had three rooms downstairs and two half-story chambers above. The home was restored and opened to visitors in October 1978. It is the only historic house museum in the country and is listed on the National Register of Historic Places.[165]

Today's horse breeding and racing, such as the Kentucky Derby, are a result of Jack Jouett, Jr.'s vision and industry.

According to Joel Meador, Executive Director of the Woodford County home site, Jouett sold the farm of 530 acres in December 1809, and moved to Bath County, Kentucky.[166]

Twenty years after his ride, when James Monroe was Governor of Virginia, Jouett received the "elegant sword" (belt, etc.[167]) promised by the Virginia General Assembly for his heroic ride on June 3, 1781. The sword was handsomely jeweled and bought from France.[168]

Jack's second son and third child, Matthew, inherited the sword presented to his father from the Virginia Legislature. Matthew's daughter remembered the children playing stick horse with the sword when she was about seven years old. That was about the time Jack Jouett, her grandfather, died at age 67.[169] Maybe the children were allowed to play "the midnight ride of Jack Jouett" with the sword.

Grayson, in her booklet, says in his old age, Jack Jouett used to laugh and say he would "do it again for another glass of Mr. Jefferson's Madeira." [170]

Jack Jouett died on March 1, 1822, in Bath County, Kentucky, either at his farm, Peeled Oak or the home of his daughter, Elizabeth Lewis Jouett Haden. He is buried in an unmarked grave probably in the family plot. His death was reported in the Lexington, Kentucky *Reporter* and the *Enquirer* of Richmond, Virginia.[171] The states of Virginia in 1940 and Kentucky in 1942, by acts of the legislature, made June 4th of each year Jack Jouett Day.[172]

The son who inherited the sword, Matthew Harris Jouett, was a captain in the War of 1812. Matthew later became a portrait painter. He studied with Gilbert Stuart in Boston. Over three hundred of his portraits survive, including those of Thomas Jefferson, Marquis de Lafayette and George Rogers Clark. Some are considered superior to those of Gilbert Stuart.[173]

A grandson of Jack Jouett, Jr., Lieutenant-Commander James Edward Jouett served in the U.S. Navy. He was stationed on the *USN Metacomet* at the Battle of Mobile Bay, during the Civil War. It was to James Jouett that Admiral Farragut directed his oft-quoted exclamation: "Damn the torpedoes, full speed ahead!" a paraphrase of the actual order, "Damn the torpedoes! Four bells. Captain Drayton, go ahead! Jouett, full speed!"[174]

Another sword

After the Battle of King's Mountain (October 7, 1780), where the British were badly beaten, General William Campbell was given a large share of the credit for the victory. He was promised a sword like Jouett. Both swords were procured by Governor James Monroe in 1803. The cost was set at a total of $300. Jouett's was delivered the same year. Campbell had been deceased for 20 years when his sword was ordered. It was therefore given to his grandson.[175]

Notes from Virginius Dabney
From Scribner's Magazine, 1928

If the career of Thomas Jefferson had been cut short in 1781, the history of the United States would be vastly different. It would have cut short the services of the man who helped build the principles upon which democracy in our Republic rests today.[176]

"What would have been the fate of men such as [Thomas] Jefferson, [Patrick] Henry, [Benjamin] Harrison, [Thomas] Nelson, Jr. and [Richard Henry] Lee, if they had fallen into British hands? They would have almost certainly been carried into captivity by Tarleton."

Dabney goes on the say, "It is hardly conceivable that men of the statue of Jefferson, Henry and the rest would have been paroled. Their capture would have been a serious blow to the morale of the Continentals, especially at a time when things were going rather badly for their cause. Incalculable, even catastrophic, results might have followed from such a coup."[177]

Dabney mentioned B.L. Raynor's "Sketches of Life, Writings, and Opinions of Thomas Jefferson," (published in 1834) that suggested the enthusiasm felt by the bloodthirsty Tarleton at the prospect of capturing the governor and legislature. He described Tarleton as elated with the idea of a raid like others he had done before. He was able and confident of an easy prey. Tarleton selected a competent body of men. Then he proceeded with ardor on his expedition.[178] Tarleton thought the raid would bring him much glory.

Remarks by Edward S. Jouett

Photographic Archives,
Ekstrom Library
University of Louisville

Edward S. Jouett (October 21, 1863-1960) was the great-grandson of Jack Jouett, Jr. He became a Vice President and General Counsel of the Louisville & Nashville Railroad and was Chairman of the Board of Trustees of the University of Louisville in Kentucky.

Edward believed if Jack Jouett, Jr. had not ridden his horse through the night on June 3, 1781, British Lieutenant Colonel Banastre Tarleton would have captured Governor Thomas Jefferson and all of the General Assemblymen-lawmakers of Virginia. Tarleton was intent and ruthless. He would take any steps necessary to carry out Cornwallis' orders.[179]

Jouett prevented the capture of many patriots

Signers of the Declaration of Independence like Thomas Jefferson, Richard Henry Lee, Benjamin Harrison, and Thomas Nelson, Jr. and orator Patrick Henry would have been shipped to England for

65

punishment. Their capture would have provided Cornwallis with great prestige and glory from King George III and the British public. Sending those patriots to England would have accomplished the greatest injury to the American cause. Cornwallis would not have overlooked this value to his military career.[180]

The careful and extensive plans Cornwallis made for their capture is proof he had some important purpose in view for their treatment.[181] The capture of the same men a few years earlier would have brought them lighter punishment. However, after six long years of resistance, the British were tired of the war, the financial drain and loss of British lives.[182]

It is not unreasonable for some students of history to feel the capture of the Revolutionary leaders, at this critical time in the war, would have been difficult to overcome. It might have caused the patriots to accept a compromise settlement that would have made the creation of the United States impossible.[183]

Author's note: As an example of possible punishment for the above mentioned men, General William Woodford, taken at the fall of Charleston in April 1780, died on a prison ship in New York harbor. He was only one of thousands to die that way. Another example of a captured patriot was Henry Laurens, President of the American Continental Congress. He went to Europe on a diplomatic mission in September 1780. The Royal Navy captured him, and he was imprisoned in the Tower of London. Held over a year, he was not abusively treated although his health suffered. He was eventually exchanged for Cornwallis after the British defeat at Yorktown.[184]

Jefferson had told the General Assembly he did not want to serve another term as governor. He would not serve if chosen. He strongly favored a military man and recommended General Thomas Nelson, Jr. At this time the legislature selected the governor.

The capture of General Nelson, elected as governor in Staunton on June 12, would have been a financial and a military loss. Nelson also possessed large private wealth. He was the leader of private citizens in providing needed arms, supplies and other support for the patriot troops in Virginia. This was especially true after the state became the main theater of war.[185]

Edward Jouett thought it was obvious that with the governor and legislature captured, Virginia would have had no leadership at all for a time. Even if new leaders could have been elected, the demoralizing effects of the disruption would have persisted much longer.[186]

Taking a larger look, Mr. Jouett considered the terrible loss and blow to the morale of the whole people of the young country and the Continental military forces. The men saved by Jack Jouett's ride were not just Virginians serving the state. Some were serving in the Continental Congress. Many other Virginians were continental officers and soldiers fighting with other colonists in other parts of the country.

At this time the war was going into its seventh year and the fighting was at a stalemate in the north. American finances were low and enlistments were down. At the same time, the British continued to have well-trained and well-equipped soldiers coming from overseas. Many discouraged colonists favored a negotiated peace.[187]

Thoughts from an early DAR historian:

"The ride was the greatest act of Jack Jouett's life. Seldom has it been equaled in the history of the world. And never, we believe, has there been more at stake than on that momentous fourth of June. Mr. Jefferson would have been taken in fetters to England and doubtless have died an arch traitor to the King. Perhaps there would have been no United States and certainly there would have been no University of Virginia."[188]—Jennie Thornley Grayson, 1922.

Jack Jouett: Revolutionary Rider

Historians' Thoughts about Jack Jouett's Ride

Stuart G. Gibboney, President of the Thomas Jefferson Memorial Foundation in 1929, said, "But for Captain Jack Jouett's heroic ride, there would have been no Yorktown and the Revolutionists would have been only unsuccessful rebels."[189]

"[M]easured by its results [the American Revolution] is the most important war in history. It was the travail of which was born the union of the Thirteen Colonies, weak dependencies of Britain, into one great republic, now the most powerful nation on earth and the sole hope of saving the world from impending political chaos."[190] —Edward S. Jouett, 1950

"Jack Jouett's thoughts can only be imagined as he espied the enemy raiders. Disregarding his own safety, however, the Virginian was immediately concerned for his country and his country's government. Fortunately, his bay mare Sally—'the fleetest steed in seven counties' was nearby in the tavern's paddock."[191]—Rick Britton, 2003

Benjamin Harrison, was quoted in a letter from Continental Congressman Joseph Jones to General George Washington on June 20, when he wrote, "Without that warning, not one man of those in town would have escaped."[192]—Michael Kranish, 2010

"It was plain that the governor and legislature would be seized unless he [Jouett] could warn them of the impending danger."[193]—Virginius Dabney, 1928

"The Old Dominion's fate was resting on his skills, the evening's visibility and [his horse] Sally's speed."[194]—Rick Britton, 2011

"Jouett was determined to beat Tarleton or die in the effort."[195] —Rick Britton 2013

"Had Jack Jouett not frustrated Tarleton's foray, a disheartening and even fatal blow might have been occasioned by the simultaneous capture of Jefferson, Henry and three signers of the Declaration of Independence at a juncture when continental fortunes were at critical ebb."[197]—Ed Crews, 2006

"Because of Jouett's quick action, knowledge of the country and superb horsemanship, leaders important not only to Virginia but to the American republic escaped the enemy's grasp."[198]—Alf J. Mapp, Jr., 1987

"After a lightning ride westward, Tarleton, whose courage, daring and insolence made him a feared enemy, was seen by Jouett, a bear of a man, who was as fearless a horseman as Tarleton himself."[199]— Jack McLaughlin, 1988

"Jouett's ride on the night of June 3, 1781, was when the fortunes of the colonists appeared to be ebbing sadly."[200]—Virginius Dabney, 1966

"...Jefferson escaped, but just barely."[201]—James L. Nelson, 2010

"On June 15, eleven days after his ride, the Virginia General Assembly voted to reward Jouett for his service with an elegant sword and a brace of pistols."[202]—Virginius Dabney, 1961

"Thanks to Jouett's warning, most members of the General Assembly already had left for Staunton over the Blue Ridge Mountains [when Tarleton arrived]."[203]—John Maass, 2000

"...a hulking American captain named Jack Jouett rode on a mission that would have challenged the stamina of Paul Revere. Jouett left Cuckoo Tavern and rode forty miles to warn Thomas Jefferson that the British were coming to seize him."[204]—A.J. Langguth, 1989

Timeline: Jack Jouett: Revolutionary Rider

The Battle of Saratoga in 1777 was a very significant victory for the American colonies. When British General John Burgoyne surrendered on October 17, 1777 at the Battle of Saratoga, two major events occurred that changed the war.

Eight months later, in July 1778, France agreed to support the American cause and declared war on Britain. Then France, Holland and Spain's alliances with the colonies turned the local rebellion into a world war. Fighting took place in the West Indies, Africa and India. England feared an invasion by the allied forces of France and Spain and worried about their colonies in the West Indies.

The other event was that with Burgoyne captured and General William Howe resigned, General Henry Clinton was chosen to replace Howe as commander of British forces in America.

Clinton's promotion made him responsible for all ground troops in the colonies. He had a career characterized by an inability to get along with his fellow commanders.[205] In America, he became frustrated with the lack of attention and support from officials in London. He tried to resign. His resignation was not accepted. Cornwallis was frustrated because he wanted to take Clinton's place.[206]

As the commander, Clinton realized the quickest way to end the rebellion was to cut off supplies on which the rebelling troops subsisted. Between one-third and one-half of those supplies came from Virginia, therefore Clinton said, Virginia should be destroyed.[207]

In May 1779, the Virginia legislature passed the Act for the Removal of the Seat of Government, deciding that Richmond would make a safer and better capital than Williamsburg.[208]

The October 4 to December 24, 1779 General Assembly Legislative Session was the last Session that met in Williamsburg.[209]

The next three Sessions were held in Richmond where the state business was conducted in a warehouse. Those sessions took place May 1 to July 14, 1780; October 16, 1780 to January 2, 1781; and March 1 to March 22, 1781.[210] The use of the old building continued into the 1780s.[211]

On May 7, 1781, the British army was moving close to Richmond. The Clerk of the House of Delegates of the Virginia General Assembly recorded that a session was held for the purpose of discussing when to leave Richmond for a safer location for their meetings. So few gentlemen attended, a quorum could not be reached. The same was true on May 8 and 9.[212]

On May 10, the General Assembly, without a quorum, resolved to adjourn until Thursday May 24. They would move to Charlottesville, in Albemarle County. Governor Jefferson attended each day's Session and remained in Richmond after the others left.[213]

General Cornwallis, on May 20, entered Virginia from North Carolina and took command of deceased General William Phillips' troops.

On May 21, Governor Jefferson and his staff reached Charlottesville.[214] British General Alexander Leslie arrived in Portsmouth on May 24 with reinforcements for Cornwallis from General Henry Clinton in New York.[215] The Virginia General

Assembly met in Charlottesville that day, and Daniel Boone was sworn in as a Delegate.

British General Benedict Arnold left Virginia on May 27 from his Turkey Island camp on the James River near Westover. He returned to New York for personal business.[216] Cornwallis took command of his army.

On May 28, Governor Thomas Jefferson acted on the assumption that Virginia had become the main theater of the war. He wrote General George Washington saying he needed the General to come to Virginia to help defend the state. Washington sent General Marquis de Lafayette with about 1,200 men to Virginia to answer Jefferson's request. Cornwallis would have about 7,000 men.

On June 2, Jefferson's term as governor expired. Because he said he would not accept reelection, he assumed he was out of office.

The election of a new governor was to take place on Saturday, June 2. Jefferson wrote some last official letters that day. The election was postponed until Monday, June 4. The Council of State could not meet to elect a governor because there were not enough members present.[217]

On June 4, after receiving the warning from Jack Jouett of Tarleton's raid, the General Assembly decided to meet in Staunton from June 7 until June 23. The Assembly adjourned and left town.

On June 7, Cornwallis arrived at Thomas Jefferson's Elk Hill farm in Goochland County. He would remain there for eight days.

American General Anthony Wayne joined Lafayette on June 10 at his encampment at Raccoon Ford north of Richmond. He brought 900 men, three regiments of Pennsylvania Continentals and one hundred continental artillerymen (sent by General Washington).[218] Those men and some state militia brought the American forces to 4,000.[219]

General Thomas Nelson, Jr. was elected governor on June 12 to replace Jefferson. Nelson was sworn in on June 18 and took leadership when the state was in terrible condition because of the British raids. He was gifted in organizational and leadership skills. On his shoulders would rest making preparations for the arrival of Washington's and Rochambeau's armies and accommodating them.

In Staunton the General Assembly wondered how they would ever recover from the devastation of the enemy's raids. They also wondered why they were not better prepared. The General Assembly voted to look into the conduct of Jefferson, as the Executive of State, for the previous twelve months. No specific charges were ever brought forth at this or any other time. The inquiry was about Arnold's raid and why the state was not prepared for that invasion. Of concern also was why the militia had not been called out. The inquiry was voted for by both Jefferson's friends and his enemies.[220]

Cornwallis left Elk Hill for Richmond on June 15, 1781. He arrived there on June 16.[221] Four days later on June 20, Cornwallis left the devastated capital.

General Baron von Steuben[222] joined Lafayette and General Wayne on June 17. Together they eventually managed to fatigue the British army, not by fighting, but constantly retreating. Cornwallis finally chose to return to the coast where his army could rest and be resupplied by British warships.

On July 4, Lafayette celebrated the signing of the Declaration of Independence with a review of his troops and dinner for his officers at Tyree's Plantation in New Kent County. Cornwallis, twenty miles away, was probably not celebrating the holiday.

On July 6, the last large battle before the British moved to and fortified Yorktown occurred at Green Spring near Jamestown (and outside of Williamsburg) on the James River.

On August 1, Cornwallis and part of his army arrived at Yorktown.

On August 14, General Washington received assurances that French Admiral Comte de Grasse would sail his fleet from the West Indies to the Chesapeake Bay.[223]

Washington and Rochambeau quietly slipped away from the British forces in New York and headed for Yorktown.

With the large British army unable to escape from Yorktown or get reinforcements, General Lord Cornwallis was forced to surrender on October 19, 1781. Washington and his army returned north to the stalemate against Clinton in New York.

The next Virginia General Assembly Session was held in Richmond from October 1, 1781 to January 5, 1782.[224] It lasted longer than usual. On December 12, Jefferson defended his official decisions even though no information had been submitted to give reason for the inquiry into his actions during his time as governor.

Both houses of government made resolutions the next week to thank Jefferson for his service to the state.[225] The Session met during the British surrender at Yorktown and the aftereffects of that great event.[226]

Years later during Jefferson's presidential campaign, these issues and his escape at Monticello from Tarleton were used in an attempt show he was not a good executive and was a coward who ran away when the state needed his services.

"Seldom has [Jouett's ride] been equaled in the history of the world. And never, has there been more at stake than on that momentous forth of June."—Virginius. Dabney, 1961

The Albemarle Barracks

The American victory over British General John Burgoyne's combined British and Hessian forces at Saratoga (October 17, 1777) had many good results for the Americans. However, it presented a problem of where to house the surrendered soldiers. The patriots had initially agreed to send the enemy soldiers back to England on the condition they would never fight the colonies again. Congress agreed that would be impossible to enforce. About 1,100 prisoners were sent to Canada, with the remaining 4,100 becoming the "Convention Army." They were moved to barracks near Boston. In November 1778, Congress ordered the Convention Army moved from Massachusetts. They cited a shortage of provisions in the area and the northern location was too vulnerable for possible rescue by British forces.[227]

Thomas Jefferson, Colonel Theodorick Bland and the Virginia delegation in Congress were instrumental in getting the Albemarle Barracks prison started outside of Charlottesville, Virginia. Jefferson thought money spent by the soldiers would help businesses in the Charlottesville area.[228]

John Harvie, who owned land in Albemarle County, offered a site located on the northern bank of Ivy Creek that occupied the top and brow of a very high hill. The camp was located far enough from the fighting to be safe from enemy troops rescuing the prisoners. The prison was situated northwest of and a few miles from Monticello.[229]

When the British and Hessian armies surrendered, they agreed officers would stay with their men. General William Phillips commanded the British troops and Baron von Riedesel the Hessian soldiers. In November 1778, the march started off badly as Boston residents taunted them as they marched out of Massachusetts.[230]

On the trip down officers and men were separated. This was done knowing it would encourage desertions. An estimated 350 men were lost to disease, exchange, or desertion. The bad weather continued and after an extremely cold march of 623 miles, about 3,750 men equally divided between Hessian and British, all short of rations, arrived in Charlottesville in January 1779.[231]

In Virginia they found the barracks unfinished, having side walls started but no roofs. The buildings were filled with snow. There was little in the way of food waiting for them.[232] Many of the discouraged prisoners would have chosen to camp in the woods.[233]

What little baggage they had sent was delayed. When it did arrive in Richmond, it was spoiled and much of it was missing. Many of the soldiers had gone two years without being issued new clothes. Like the American men, many were without shoes and thinly clad.[234]

This must have been extra hard on the Hessian soldiers who were mostly sent to America against their will. Frederick II of Prussia was receiving 100,000 pounds a year plus 30 crowns per soldier for their service from England. The men had been assured the Americans would be easily defeated and they would win glory and treasure for their service.[235]

Prisoners were ordered by their officers to finish the buildings and later to plant gardens and corral livestock. The barracks were organized in four rows of twelve houses in closely connected squares. Each house held eighteen men.[236]

Through the efforts of the prisoners themselves, their conditions greatly improved. The prison eventually had its own store, coffee house, large church and tavern. Four houses of entertainment were built by a local man and equipped with billiard tables.[237]

At one time during the encampment, Edgar Woods, an early Charlottesville historian, stated in "the space of more than three months there have been but four deaths, two infants under three weeks of age and two others by apoplexy [stroke]. The officers said the troops were never so healthy since they were embodied." There were also women and children camp followers who traveled with the soldiers.[238]

With so few guards, the Virginians were helpless to stop escapes. The prison population shrank to about three thousand men. Many Hessians escaped and settled in the Blue Ridge Mountains in Virginia where they were gladly accepted into existing German settlements.[239] Some British soldiers made their way back to British forces.

The British and Hessian officers were allowed to reside within a one-hundred-mile radius of Charlottesville in rented houses or as guest of residents.

Many of the wealthy residents entertained British and Hessian officers, whose presence added new enlightenments to the area's social circles. The officers had freedom of movement to enjoy culture, conversations and music. Jefferson and other landed families enjoyed the company of several of these officers including the Hessian Commander Riedesel and British General Phillips, who was later exchanged, invaded Virginia, then died in Petersburg in 1781.[240] Jefferson was elated when he found Hessian musicians among the prisoners. One in particular, Friedrick Wilhelm von Geismar, was an accomplished violinist who joined Jefferson on his violin with Mrs. Jefferson accompanying on her pianoforte. There was also the elegantly dressed Baroness Riedesel leading the dances.[241]

Officers were given passes to travel to other places in the region such as Richmond and Hampton. All of this was done disregarding the concerns of fellow Virginians who saw the possibility of these foreign officers becoming familiar with the land, roads and gathering other intelligence. That information would be helpful when these officers were exchanged and leading armies again.[242]

Life must have settled into a somewhat relaxed pattern for the soldiers, until the fall of 1780, when the British invaded Virginia by water in the months before Benedict Arnold arrived. With the possibility of a British invasion reaching Charlottesville and with Tory conspiracies unearthed in the southwest part of the state that posed a threat of liberating the Convention Army,[243] Jefferson wisely had the prisoners moved to Maryland. It might have been the final blow if the Convention Army had been kept in Charlottesville and Tarleton had released them. They would have greatly increased the size of his army. There were some twenty Hessians who managed to hide in the woods near the Albemarle Barracks prison. They found their way to Tarleton's men before he left in June 1781.[244]

Hessian room at Silver Thatch Inn in Charlottesville

One of the few remaining Hessian officers' houses showing American chestnut log walls and yellow pine floors.

Latitude 38.095089N – Longitude 79.525949W
Located on Barracks Farm Road (St. Rt. 658)
Charlottesville, Virginia

Mountain Road/Three Notch'd Road

A portion of Jack Jouett's ride was on Old Mountain Road (present Route 640). A section of that route is now called Jack Jouett Road.

Jack also used a portion of Three Notch'd Road (Route 250). That road was originally started when Goochland County Court ordered a "new" road on June 19, 1733. In the spring of 1734, Peter Jefferson, father of Thomas, became the surveyor. This new road was to go from the mountains, down the ridge between the Rivanna and the South Anna Rivers. It followed an Indian trail used by foot travelers and animals as they moved through the wilderness. In those early days a road was cut or opened more than once before a satisfactory dirt surface was produced.

Three Notch'd Road became the main connector from the Blue Ridge Mountains to Richmond and helped settle Albemarle County and the Southwest Mountains. During the first decade, it was known as Mountain or Mountain Ridge Road.[245]

By 1745 the road was open from the Blue Ridge Mountains to Richmond. Marked, probably by Peter Jefferson, it had three notches on trees at regular intervals. Miles were marked going from the west toward the east. Mile number 12 was near Shadwell (at the bottom of the mountain from Monticello) and numbers 36 and 40 were near Goochland Court House. The road became known as Three Notch'd (later Three Chopt or Chopped) Road. The fact that it had the miles marked shows it was important. Another road in the area had two chops and a cross to mark it.[246]

Early Three Notch'd Road in Eastern Goochland County
Virginia Center for Transportation Innovation & Research

Early Three Notch'd Road near Richmond circa 1970
Virginia Center for Transportation Innovation & Research

Later a road went from Staunton through Rockfish Gap to Ivy Creek in Albemarle County. Ivy Creek was mentioned near the Albemarle Barracks outside of Charlottesville. It became part of Three Notch'd Road.[247] The road appears on a map by William Faden in the 1787 edition of Banastre Tarleton's book *A History of the Campaigns of 1780-1781 in the Southern Provinces of North America.*[248]

There were many colonial roads constructed during this time period. Some of them can be located on maps prepared later by Confederate engineers.[249] Three Notch'd Road was one of the most significant and remained virtually intact and in service for two hundred years as a state road from the 1730s until the 1930s.

It was superseded by U.S. Route 250 in the 1930s. The new route straightened the older road. The newest route, Interstate 64, follows the same Three Notch'd Road. It crosses the Rivanna River closer to Secretary's Ford. That was where Tarleton skirmished with militia to cross the river and enter Charlottesville.[250] In Charlottesville the original course of Three Notch'd Road is found on west Main Street and part of University Avenue.

The Marquis de Lafayette later used the Old Mountain Road Route 640 to take a defensive stance at Giles Allegre's Tavern near the Mechunk Creek, thus blocking the British advance and saving munitions stored at Albemarle Old Courthouse near Scottsville.[251]

Captain Christopher Hudson's statement
July 26, 1805

"In the month of June 1781-------------[?] on my way to join the Marquis de Lafayette's army, I met with a Mr. Long, who informed me that Mr. Duoit [Jouett] had arrived the preceding evening at Charlottesville & brought information of the approach of the English to that place under Tarleton, upon inquiring from Long as to whether Mr. Jefferson had received information he was ignorant. I immediately proceeded to Monticello where I found Mr. Jefferson perfectly tranquil & undisturbed, at my earnest request he left his house, which was surrounded in ten minutes at farthest by a troop of Light horse, I was convinced his situation was truly critical since there was only one man (his gardener) upon the Spot. I well remember he was not governor at that time, his term of service having expired & General Nelson appointed his successor.

I was also attached to Capt. Call's troop of horse when Phipps [Philips] & Arnold in their second invasion of Virginia reached Manchester. I was constantly on duty, where Mr. Jefferson (then Governor) always appeared & by his presence, activity & perfect composure, inspired the troops with the utmost confidence; he remained in Richmond until the retreat of the English to Warwick & down James River."

Christopher Hudson.

Signed by Captain Hudson in presence of Isaac Coles and William A. Burwell [252]

Personal accounts

Three men traveled together from Richmond to Charlottesville, as the Virginia General Assembly moved to conduct business away from British interference. First was Irish-born Peter Lyons, a physically large man and a judge on the General Court of Virginia. Second was Colonel John Syme of Hanover County, a member of the House of Delegates of the Virginia General Assembly and a half-brother of Patrick Henry. The third man was Newman Brockenbrough, a member of the House of Delegates from Essex County.

When warned that the British might be near Charlottesville and Castle Hill (home of Dr. Thomas Walker), Colonel Syme assured the other men they were safe because the British would not come that far west. A scout went to look for signs of the approaching British. The scout found no proof the enemy was coming.[253]

These men didn't know a message had been sent to Dr. Walker from a neighbor, telling him of Tarleton's approach. The message was intercepted by a British officer who gave it to Colonel Tarleton. That informed Tarleton important people were staying at Castle Hill.[254]

Judge Lyons later recalled, "We indulged the thoughts of being far from the enemy and the pleasure of a good night's repose." They enjoyed a meal and a half night's sleep. Very early in the morning, Dr. Walker suddenly awoke them. It was before dawn, but some moonlight was available. Judge Lyons got out of bed. "Looking out of the window, I saw the yard and house surrounded with enemy soldiers, so that an attempt to get away was useless."[255]

When Mr. Brockenbrough went downstairs, he found Tarleton had control of the house. Mr. Brockenbrough asked to be released because of his health. Tarleton said because he was a Delegate to the General Assembly, he was too valuable to release.[256]

Judge Lyons had gone back to bed, so when the soldiers took him from his room, he was not ready. When he appeared outdoors, half-dressed and very overweight, the British soldiers laughed at him. Tarleton decided he would be too much trouble to try to take with them. He was released.[257]

The story continues

Judge Syme, like Brockenbrough, must not have gone to Staunton after he was released. His name does not appear on the attendance records until the legislature met in Richmond in October 1781.[258]

Later in 1784, three years after the event of Tarleton's raid, Newman Brockenbrough was accused of going to the British voluntarily. The accusers said it could be proved that enough notice was given to Doctor Walker for the men to make an escape before the enemy actually arrived. (Those making the charges about Brockenbrough didn't know the message had been intercepted by Tarleton's men, and Dr. Walker never got the warning.) Lastly, Brockenbrough was said to have enjoyed dining with Lord Cornwallis and received presents of a considerable amount, an elegant horse and much clothing from the British. Brockenbrough's letter asking for help to clear his name appeared in the Richmond *Virginia Gazette or, the American Advertiser* on September 18, 1784. To clear himself of the charges, Brockenbrough asked Colonel Syme and Judge Lyons to write what they remembered about the events that occurred when Tarleton had captured the three men. There is only one response available; if Colonel Syme answered, his letter has not been found.[259]

Some additional light on the issue might be that Brockenbrough had a brother named Austin who was a loyalist and went to England during the war, only to return after the war ended. Another brother, Dr. John Brockenbrough of Tappahannock, was also accused of loyalist inclinations.[260]

In answering, Judge Lyons said in his letter they had stopped by the home of a relative because the weather was inclement. They stayed a couple of days until the weather improved. On Saturday, June 2, John Walker came to the house and told them of a report that the enemy was advancing. He also said that if Brockenbrough was captured, he would receive severe punishment because of the seat he held in the House of Delegates. Walker suggested they move on to Charlottesville as soon as possible. The men set out early the next day, Sunday morning, June 3, expecting to go to Charlottesville.[261]

During the day, they stopped by Colonel John Syme's house to learn what he knew of the enemy's movements. Colonel Syme had come from Charlottesville the day before (Saturday, June 2). He thought the report of the enemy moving their way was not well founded. He also reported the Assemblymen had little fear of the enemy coming so far west and they were expecting to meet the next morning (Monday) in Charlottesville. Syme said that if they would accompany him to Dr. Walker's home, then he would go with them to Charlottesville. The three agreed and stopped for the night at Dr. Walker's home on the June 3.[262] The next day, Judge Lyons said, "Dr. Walker came very early into our chamber and told us the British were there, but desired us to lie still and perhaps we might escape being discovered."[263]

"On looking out the window, I [Judge Lyon] saw the yard and house surrounded with soldiers, so that an attempt to get away was useless. I therefore lay down, but you proceeded to dress, so that when we were called down, which happened soon after, you went some time before I was ready." After Judge Lyon went down and saw Colonel

Tarleton, "you [Brockenbrough] asked me if I knew what they were going to do with me. I told you I did not and enquired if you knew your own fate?"[264]

"You [Brockenbrough] said Colonel Tarleton would not parole you because of the position of Delegate you held. ...I well remember when he [Tarleton] was going off, he ordered an officer to take charge of you and carry you on..."[265]

Judge Lyons was not taken, but his son, James, was captured the same day. After James was released and returned home, he said that "Lord Cornwallis paroled you [Brockenbrough] as soon as you got to camp. I understand that Lord Cornwallis expressed surprise that Tarleton should go to the trouble of taking the men prisoner."[266]

"As for civility, we all received much more of it, than we expected; but your treatment was rather rigid, in being dragged so far from camp, when you were scarce able to ride..."[267]

John Cook Wyllie closed the above article with the final remarks by the Judge. "... for however people might differ about the war, or the mode of conducting it while it lasted, surely now there is peace, all should unite zealously in promoting and preserving it and this I conceive must be the ardent wish of every good man and if anything I have written ...will help you ...it will give me infinite pleasure."

Historical Highway Markers
Related to Jack Jouett's Ride

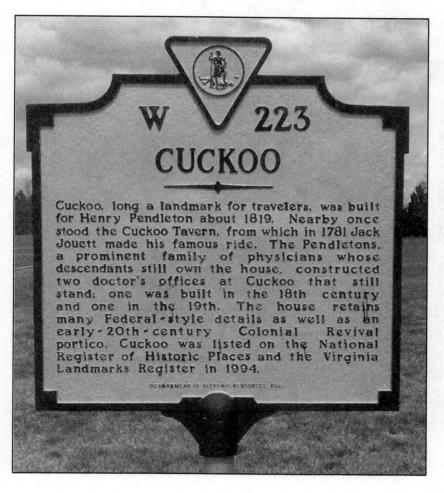

Located at Cuckoo, Virginia on State Route 522
Latitude 37.953835N– Longitude 77.900576W

Located at Cuckoo, Virginia on State Route 522
Latitude 37.953835N– Longitude 77900576W

Located in the Town of Louisa on State Route 33
Latitude 38.021864N– Longitude 77.999257W

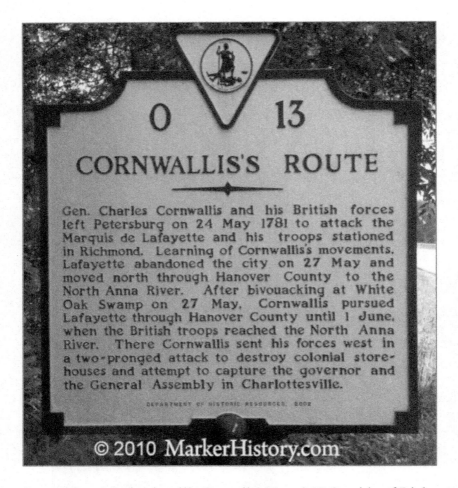

Located on Mechanicsville Turnpike Hwy 360 Outside of Richmond
Latitude 37.6813957N – Longitude 77.1884055W

Picture courtesy of MarkerHistory.com
http://www.markerhistory.com/cornwalliss-route-marker-o-13/

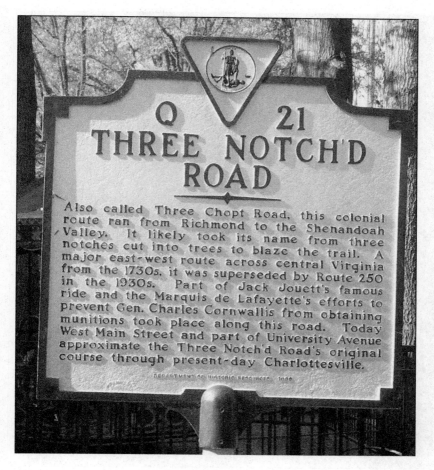

Located downtown, East Main Street, Charlottesville, Virginia
Latitude 38.029601N– Longitude 78.477761W

Located at Courthouse Square, Charlottesville, Virginia
Latitude 38.031854N – Longitude 78.477384W

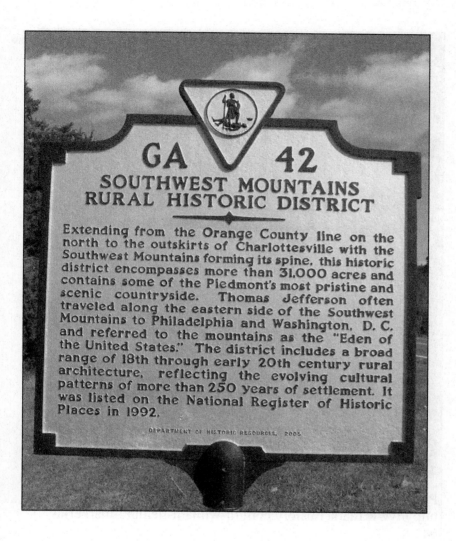

Located on Stony Point Road, Rivanna, Virginia
Latitude 38.115631N – Longitude 78.347031W

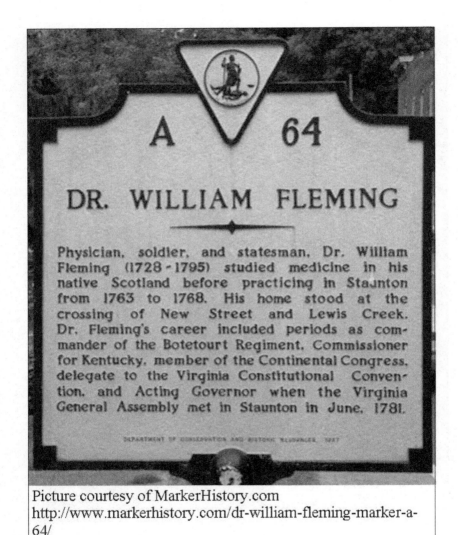

Picture courtesy of MarkerHistory.com
http://www.markerhistory.com/dr-william-fleming-marker-a-64/

South New Street, Staunton, Virginia
Latitude 38.14840175N – Longitude 79.07130851W

Endnotes

[1] The population of the Virginia Colony in 1780 was 583,000. The next largest colony was Pennsylvania with a population of 327,300. Massachusetts (including Maine) had 318,500 people. Information was taken from Bart McDowell, *The Revolutionary War* (Washington: National Geographic Society, 1967), 196.
[2] John Maass, "To Disturb the Assembly," *Virginia Cavalcade* (Autumn 2000): 150.
[3] John Selby, *The Revolution in Virginia 1775-1783* (Williamsburg: The Colonial Williamsburg Foundation, 1988), 163.
[4] Michael Kranish, *Flight from Monticello: Thomas Jefferson at War* (New York: Oxford University Press, 2010), 260.
[5] Kranish, *Flight from Monticello*, 260.
[6] Maass, *Revolution in Virginia*, 150.
[7] Lord George Germain was British Secretary of State for the American Colonies and the civilian overseer and chief architect of the war in America.
[8] Kranish, *Flight from Monticello,* 260.
[9] Virginius Dabney, "From Cuckoo Tavern to Monticello," *The Iron Worker* (Summer 1966): 1.
[10] Kranish, *Flight from Monticello*, 127.
[11] Kranish, *Flight from Monticello*, fn #3 on 349.
[12] Kranish, *Flight from Monticello*, 128.
[13] "Mourning Glenn Harris," Leanne Cragun's Family History [database online] http://www.cragun.com/leanne/ getperson.php?personID=I688&tree=Dalling Accessed 7/29/2014.
[14] Jennie Thornley Grayson, *Jack Jouett of Albemarle: The Paul Revere of Virginia* (Charlottesville: Daughters of the American Revolution, Jack Jouett Chapter, 1922), 3.

[15] Kranish, *Flight from Monticello*, 275.

[16] Grayson, *Jack Jouett of Albemarle*, 2.

[17] Edgar Woods, *Albemarle County in Virginia* (Charlottesville: The Michie Company Printers, 1901), 29.

[18] Rick Britton, "From Cuckoo to Charlottesville: Jack Jouett's Overnight Ride," *Journal of the American Revolution* (March 5, 2013) http://allthingsliberty.com/2013/03/from-cuckoo-to-charlottesville-jack-jouetts-overnight-ride/.

[19] *Wikipedia.org*, s.v. "Jack Jouett."

[20] *Sackville King's Ordinary*. https://sites.google.com/site/kinggenealogy/sackvilleking%27sordinary.

[21] Dabney, "From Cuckoo Tavern," 2.

[22] Selby, *Revolution in Virginia 1775-1783*, 213.

[23] Virginius Dabney, *The New Dominion* (New York: Doubleday & Company, 1971), 152.

[24] Bryan Conrad, "Lafayette and Cornwallis in Virginia, 1781," *William and Mary College Quarterly Historical Magazine, 2nd series* 14, no. 2 (1934): 102.

[25] Maass, *Revolution in Virginia*, 153.

[26] Virginius Dabney, "Jack Jouett's Ride," *American Heritage Magazine* 13, no. 1 (1961): 56-59. http://americanheritage.com.

[27] Ed Crews, "Captain Jack Jouett's Ride to Rescue," *The Journal of the Colonial Williamsburg Foundation* 28, no. 3 (2006): 4.

[28] James Breig, "Williamsburg Moves to Richmond," *The Journal of the Colonial Williamsburg Foundation* 35, no. 5 (2013): 54.

[29] Kranish, *Flight from Monticello*, 269.

[30] Edward O. McCue, III, *A Jouett Miscellany* unpublished notes. Albemarle and Charlottesville, Virginia Historical Society (March 1981): 2.

[31] Selby, *Revolution in Virginia 1775-1783*, 276.

[32] Conrad, "Lafayette and Cornwallis," 102.

[33] Selby, *Revolution in Virginia 1775-1783*, 276.

[34] Selby, *Revolution in Virginia 1775-1783*, 276.

[35] Selby, *Revolution in Virginia 1775-1783*, 277.
[36] Kranish, *Flight from Monticello*, 274.
[37] Britton, "From Cuckoo to Charlottesville."
[38] Banastre Tarleton, *A History of the Campaigns of 1780 and 1781, in the Southern Provinces of North America* (London: T. Cadell, 1787), 194.
[39] Tarleton, *Campaigns of 1780 and 1781*, 295.
[40] Maass, *Revolution in Virginia*, 153.
[41] Tarleton, *Campaigns of 1780 and 1781*, 296.
[42] Tarleton, *Campaigns of 1780 and 1781*, 296.
[43] Kranish, *Flight from Monticello*, 276.
[44] Kranish, *Flight from Monticello*, 276.
[45] Jean L. Cooper, *A Guide to Historic Charlottesville and Albemarle County Virginia* (Charleston: The History Press, 2007), 70.
[46] Kranish, *Flight from Monticello*, 276.
[47] Kranish, *Flight from Monticello*, 277.
[48] Tarleton, *Campaigns of 1780 and 1781*, 296.
[49] K. Burnell Evans, "Descendents of Jefferson neighbor reunite in Albemarle," *Charlottesville Daily Progress*, August 10, 2013, http://www.dailyprogress.com/.
[50] Dabney, "Jack Jouett's Ride."
[51] Kranish, *Flight from Monticello*, 277.
[52] Kranish, *Flight from Monticello*, 280.
[53] Kranish, *Flight from Monticello*, 281.
[54] Tarleton, *Campaigns of 1780 and 1781*, 296.
[55] Tarleton, *Campaigns of 1780 and 1781*, 296.
[56] Dabney, "Jack Jouett's Ride."
[57] Alf J. Mapp, Jr., *Thomas Jefferson, A Strange Case of Mistaken Identity* (New York: Madison Books, 1987), 154.
[58] Kranish, *Flight from Monticello*, 283.
[59] Kranish, *Flight from Monticello*, 281.
[60] Kranish, *Flight from Monticello*, 281.
[61] Rector Hudson, "Christopher Hudson Insures Thomas Jefferson's Safety," *Tyler's Quarterly Historical and Genealogical Magazine* (1940): 97.

[62] Hudson, "Christopher Hudson Insures Thomas Jefferson's Safety," 97.

[63] J. Luther Kibler, "Jack Jouett, Jr. and Christopher Hudson," *Tyler's Quarterly Historical and Genealogical Magazine* (1941): 52.

[64] Edward S. Jouett, "Jack Jouett's Ride," *Filson Club History Quarterly* 24, no. 2 (1950): 24.

[65] Dabney, "Jack Jouett's Ride."

[66] Kranish, *Flight from Monticello*, 284.

[67] Tarleton, *Campaigns of 1780 and 1781*, 297.

[68] Tarleton, *Campaigns of 1780 and 1781*, 297.

[69] Kranish, *Flight from Monticello*, 284.

[70] Kranish, *Flight from Monticello*, 284.

[71] Dabney, "Jack Jouett's Ride."

[72] Kranish. *Flight from Monticello*, 284.

[73] John Cook Wyllie, "Daniel Boone's Adventures in Charlottesville in 1781: Some Incidents Connected with Tarleton's Raid," *The Magazine of Albemarle County History* 19 (1960-61): 16.

[74] Wyllie, "Daniel Boone's Adventures," 6.

[75] Wyllie, "Daniel Boone's Adventures," 9; Robert Morgan, *Boone: a Biography* (Algonquin, NC: Algonquin Books of Chapel Hill, 2008), 303.

[76] Wyllie, "Daniel Boone's Adventures," 8-9.

[77] Dabney, "From Cuckoo Tavern," 7.

[78] Wyllie, "Daniel Boone's Adventures," 17 fn. 27.

[79] Wyllie, "Daniel Boone's Adventures," 17 fn. 27.

[80] Morgan, *Boone*, 303.

[81] Wyllie, "Daniel Boone's Adventures," 9.

[82] Wyllie, "Daniel Boone's Adventures," 9.

[83] Curtis Carroll Davis, ed., "Farewell to Fleming! Lewis Littlepage Eulogizes a Patriot," *The Virginia Magazine of History and Biography* 74, no. 4 (1966), 449; and Calder Loth, *Virginia Landmarks Register*, 3rd ed. (Charlottesville, University of Virginia Press, 1986), 175.

[84] *Wikipedia.org*, s.v. "Archibald Cary."

[85] Thomas Kindig, "Benjamin Harrison, 1726-1791," *Signers of the Declaration of Independence.* c2009-2014. http://www.ushistory.org/declaration/signers/harrison.htm; and *Wikipedia.org*, s.v. "Benjamin Harrison V."

[86] Kindig, "Benjamin Harrison, 1726-1791."

[87] *Wikipedia.org*, s.v. "Richard Henry Lee."

[88] *Wikipedia.org*, s.v. "Richard Henry Lee."

[89] Dabney, "Jack Jouett's Ride,"; Joseph Cummins, *Ten Tea Parties that History Forgot* (Philadelphia: Quirk Books, 2012), 212.

[90] *Wikipedia.org*, s.v. "Thomas Nelson, Jr."

[91] Kranish, *Flight from Monticello*, 269.

[92] *Wikipedia.org*, s.v. "Patrick Henry."

[93] *Wikipedia.org*, s.v. "Patrick Henry."

[94] Kranish, *Flight from Monticello*, 277.

[95] Grayson, *Jack Jouett of Albemarle*, 6.

[96] Dabney, "Jack Jouett's Ride,"; *Wikipedia.org*, s.v. "Edward Stevens (general)."

[97] Lawrence E. Babits and Joshua B. Howard, *Long, Obstinate, and Bloody: The Battle of Guilford Courthouse* (Chapel Hill, NC: The University of North Carolina Press, 2009), 140-141.

[98] *Wikipedia.org*, s.v. "John Tyler, Sr."

[99] John Cook Wyllie, ed., "New Documentary Light on Tarleton's Raid," *The Virginia Magazine of History and Biography* 74, no. 4 (1966): 459 fn. 10 & fn. 14.

[100] Wyllie, "New Documentary Light," 459 fn. 14.

[101] Wyllie, "New Documentary Light," 459 fn. 14.

[102] Wyllie, "New Documentary Light," 459 fn. 14.

[103] *Wikipedia.org*, s.v. "Francis Kinloch (Congressman)."

[104] Kranish, *Flight from Monticello*, 277.

[105] Wyllie, "New Documentary Light," 460 fn. 18.

[106] Wyllie, "New Documentary Light," 457 fn. 11.

[107] Wyllie, "New Documentary Light," 153 fn. 20.

[108] Wyllie, "Daniel Boone's Adventures," 13 fn. 20.

[109] "Yorktown Battlefield, Yorktown, Virginia," *A Revolutionary Day.* c2005. http://www.revolutionaryday.com/usroute60/ yorktown/

[110] Wyllie, "Daniel Boone's Adventures," 14 fn. 15.
[111] Wyllie, "Daniel Boone's Adventures," 14 fn. 15.
[112] Dabney, "From Cuckoo Tavern," 3.
[113] Wyllie, "Daniel Boone's Adventures," 14.
[114] Kranish, *Flight from Monticello*, 270.
[115] Selby, *Revolution in Virginia 1775-1783*, 273.
[116] Kranish, *Flight from Monticello*, 270.
[117] Kranish, *Flight from Monticello*, 270.
[118] David B. Mattern, *Benjamin Lincoln and the American Revolution* (Columbia: University of South Carolina, 1995), 78.
[119] Tarleton, *Campaigns of 1780 and 1781*, 65.
[120] Fitz Hirschfeld, ed., "Burnt All Their Houses," *The Virginia Magazine of History and Biography* 99, no. 4 (1991): 515.
[121] Hirschfeld, "Burnt All Their Houses," 515.
[122] Hirschfeld, "Burnt All Their Houses," 514.
[123] Hirschfeld, "Burnt All Their Houses," 513.
[124] Hirschfeld, "Burnt All Their Houses," 516.
[125] Kranish, *Flight from Monticello*, 274.
[126] Kranish, *Flight from Monticello*, 290.
[127] Selby, *Revolution in Virginia 1775-1783*, 280.
[128] Kranish, *Flight from Monticello*, 288.
[129] Dabney, "Jack Jouett's Ride."
[130] Kranish, *Flight from Monticello*, 288.
[131] Kranish, *Flight from Monticello*, 292.
[132] Kranish, *Flight from Monticello*, 291.
[133] Jean Carson, *Patrick Henry, The Prophet of the Revolution* (Williamsburg: Virginia Independence Bicentennial Commission, 1979), 43.
[134] "Trinity Church," *Little Bits of History Along U.S. Roadways.* http://littlebitsofhistory.blogspot.com/2012/12/trinity-church.html.
[135] Selby, *Revolution in Virginia 1775-1783*, 282.
[136] Selby, *Revolution in Virginia 1775-1783*, 282.
[137] Selby, *Revolution in Virginia 1775-1783*, 282.
[138] Selby, *Revolution in Virginia 1775-1783*, 283.
[139] Selby, *Revolution in Virginia 1775-1783*, 283.

140 Emory G. Evans, *Thomas Nelson of Yorktown; Revolutionary Virginian.* (Charlottesville: University Press of Virginia, 1975), 106.

141 Evans, *Thomas Nelson of Yorktown*, 106.

142 Kranish, *Flight from Monticello*, 303; and Evans, *Thomas Nelson of Yorktown*, 111.

143 Kranish, *Flight from Monticello*, 302.

144 Kranish, *Flight from Monticello*, 302-3.

145 Kranish, *Flight from Monticello*, 303.

146 Kranish, *Flight from Monticello*, 303.

147 Kranish, *Flight from Monticello*, 303 fn. 4.

148 Captain Johann Ewald, *Diary of the American War: A Hessian Journal*, trans. and ed. Joseph P. Tustin (New Haven: Yale University Press, 1979), 315.

149 Ewald, *Diary of the American War*, 315.

150 Kranish, *Flight from Monticello*, 304.

151 Evans, *Thomas Nelson of Yorktown*, 111.

152 Evans, *Thomas Nelson of Yorktown*, 106.

153 Evans, *Thomas Nelson of Yorktown*, 111.

154 Ewald, *Diary of the American War*, 315.

155 Evans, *Thomas Nelson of Yorktown*, 111.

156 Evans, *Thomas Nelson of Yorktown*, 112.

157 Evans, *Thomas Nelson of Yorktown*, 111.

158 Evans, *Thomas Nelson of Yorktown*, 112.

159 Kranish, *Flight from Monticello*, 294. There is a Windsor chair used during those meetings on display in the corner of Columba's Chapel.

160 Dabney, "From Cuckoo Tavern," 8.

161 William P. Palmer, ed., *Calendar of Virginia State Papers* (New York: Kraus Reprint Corp., 1968), v. 3, 509.

162 Mercer County was named after General Hugh Mercer, a patriot leader who died at the Battle of Princeton.

163 John Lewis RoBards, "Robards Family," *The Virginia Magazine of History and Biography* 10, no. 1 (1902): 98.

164 Woodford County was named after William Woodford, commander at the Battle of Great Bridge.

[165] Jeanmarie Andrews, "Another Famous Ride," *Early American Life* (April 2013): 49.

[166] Andrews, "Another Famous Ride," 49.

[167] Palmer, ed., *Calendar of Virginia State Papers*, v. 9, 427.

[168] Jouett, "Jack Jouett's Ride," 148.

[169] McCue, "A Jouett miscellany," 5.

[170] Grayson, *Jack Jouett of Albemarle*, 4.

[171] McCue, "A Jouett miscellany," 11.

[172] Jouett, "Jack Jouett's Ride," 153.

[173] Dabney, "From Cuckoo Tavern,"10.

[174] Dabney, "From Cuckoo Tavern," 10.

[175] Virginius Dabney, "Jouett Outrides Tarleton," *Scribner's Magazine* 83 (June 1928): 695.

[176] Dabney, "Jouett Outrides Tarleton," 697.

[177] Dabney, "Jack Jouett's Ride."

[178] Dabney, "Jouett Outrides Tarleton," 694.

[179] Jouett, "Jack Jouett's Ride," 149.

[180] Jouett, "Jack Jouett's Ride," 150.

[181] Jouett, "Jack Jouett's Ride," 143.

[182] Thomas Fleming, *What If? Watersheds, Revolutions, and Rebellions, Unlikely Victory*, ed. Robert Cowley (New York: Simon and Schuster Audioworks, 2000): Tape 1 b.

[183] Jouett, "Jack Jouett's Ride," 150.

[184] Kranish, *Flight from Monticello*, 307.

[185] Jouett, "Jack Jouett's Ride," 150.

[186] Jouett, "Jack Jouett's Ride," 151.

[187] Jouett, "Jack Jouett's Ride," 151.

[188] Grayson, *Jack Jouett of Albemarle*, 5.

[189] Donald Norman Moran, ed., "Jack Jouett of Virginia, the 'Other Ride,'" *The Valley Compatriot* (February 1984): 4. http://americanrevolution.org/jouett.html

[190] Jouett, "Jack Jouett's Ride," 142.

[191] Britton, "From Cuckoo to Charlottesville."

[192] Kranish, *Flight from Monticello*, 364.

[193] Dabney, "Jouett Outrides Tarleton," 691.

[194] Rick Britton, "Midnight rider: How Jack Jouett saved Virginia," *The Hook* no. 1019 (May 12, 2011): 4. http://www.readthehook.com/90493/overnight-ride-jack-jouett's-race-cuckoo.

[195] Britton, "From Cuckoo to Charlottesville."

[196] Removed.

[197] Ed Crews, "Captain Jack Jouett's Ride to Rescue," *The Journal of the Colonial Williamsburg Foundation* 28, no. 3 (2006): 66-71.

[198] Mapp, *Thomas Jefferson,* 154.

[199] Jack McLaughlin, *Jefferson and Monticello: The Biography of a Builder* (New York: Holt Paperbacks, 1990), 168.

[200] Dabney, "From Cuckoo Tavern," 1.

[201] James L. Nelson, *George Washington's Great Gamble* (New York: McGraw-Hill, 2010), 203.

[202] Dabney, "From Cuckoo Tavern," 8.

[203] Maass, "To Disturb the Assembly," 154.

[204] A. J. Langguth, *Patriots: the Men Who Started the American Revolution* (New York: Simon and Schuster, 1989), 514.

[205] Selby, *Revolution in Virginia 1775-1783,* 287.

[206] Nelson, *George Washington's Great Gamble,* 13.

[207] Bryan Conrad, "Lafayette and Cornwallis in Virginia, 1781," *William and Mary College Quarterly Historical Magazine, 2nd series* 14, no. 2 (1934): 100.

[208] James Breig, "Williamsburg Moves to Richmond," *The Journal of the Colonial Williamsburg Foundation* 35, no. 5 (2013): 54.

[209] Wyllie, "New Documentary Light," fn6 p. 8.

[210] Wyllie, "New Documentary Light," fn6 p. 8.

[211] Breig, "Williamsburg Moves to Richmond," 55.

[212] Kranish, *Flight from Monticello,* 256.

[213] Kranish, *Flight from Monticello,* 256.

[214] Selby, *Revolution in Virginia 1775-1783,* 277.

[215] Conrad, "Lafayette and Cornwallis in Virginia, 1781," 102.

[216] Conrad, "Lafayette and Cornwallis in Virginia, 1781," 102.

[217] Dumas Malone, *Thomas Jefferson: A Brief Biography* (Charlottesville: Thomas Jefferson Memorial Foundation, Monticello Monograph Series, 1933): 19.

[218] Harry M. Ward, and Harold E. Greer, Jr., *Richmond during the Revolution 1775-83* (Charlottesville: University Press of Virginia, 1977), 92.

[219] Selby, *Revolution in Virginia 1775-1783*, 286.

[220] Malone, *Thomas Jefferson*, 19.

[221] Selby, *Revolution in Virginia 1775-1783*, 289.

[222] Selby, *Revolution in Virginia 1775-1783*, 289.

[223] Kranish, *Flight from Monticello*, 306.

[224] Wyllie, "Daniel Boone's Adventures," fn. 6, p 8.

[225] Malone, *Thomas Jefferson*, 19-20.

[226] Wyllie, "Daniel Boone's Adventures," 8.

[227] Kranish, *Flight from Monticello*, 105.

[228] Kranish, *Flight from Monticello*, 105.

[229] Kranish, *Flight from Monticello*, 105.

[230] Kranish, *Flight from Monticello*, 105.

[231] Ward & Greer, *Richmond during the Revolution*, 105.

[232] Kranish, *Flight from Monticello*, 107.

[233] Kranish, *Flight from Monticello*, 107.

[234] Ward & Greer, *Richmond during the Revolution*, 106.

[235] Kranish, *Flight from Monticello*, 106.

[236] Kranish, *Flight from Monticello*, 108.

[237] Kranish, *Flight from Monticello*, 109.

[238] Woods, *Albemarle County in Virginia*, 32.

[239] Ward & Greer, *Richmond during the Revolution*, 106.

[240] Ward & Greer, *Richmond during the Revolution*, 106.

[241] Kranish, *Flight from Monticello*, 112.

[242] Selby, *Revolution in Virginia 1775-1783*, 219.

[243] Selby, *Revolution in Virginia 1775-1783*, 219.

[244] Kranish, *Flight from Monticello*, 281.

[245] Nathaniel M. Pawlett and Howard H. Newlon, Jr., *The Route of Three Notch'd Road: A Preliminary Report*. Rev. ed. (Richmond, VA: Virginia Department of Transportation, 2003), 7.

[246] Pawlett & Newlon, *Route of Three Notch'd Road*, 7.

[247] Pawlett & Newlon, *Route of Three Notch'd Road*, 8.

[248] Pawlett & Newlon, *Route of Three Notch'd Road*, 10.

[249] Pawlett & Newlon, *Route of Three Notch'd Road*, 3.

[250] Pawlett & Newlon, *Route of Three Notch'd Road*, 10.

[251] Pawlett & Newlon, *Route of Three Notch'd Road*, 7.

[252] Christopher Hudson, "Statement of Christopher Hudson," *William and Mary Quarterly, 2nd series* 20, no. 1 (1940): 113.

[253] Kranish, *Flight from Monticello*, 276.

[254] Kranish, *Flight from Monticello*, 276.

[255] Kranish, *Flight from Monticello*, 277.

[256] Kranish, *Flight from Monticello*, 277.

[257] Kranish, *Flight from Monticello*, 277.

[258] Wyllie, "New Documentary Light," 456.

[259] Wyllie, "New Documentary Light," 455.

[260] Wyllie, "New Documentary Light," 453.

[261] Wyllie, "New Documentary Light," 459.

[262] Wyllie, "New Documentary Light," 460.

[263] Wyllie, "New Documentary Light," 460.

[264] Wyllie, "New Documentary Light," 460.

[265] Wyllie, "New Documentary Light," 460.

[266] Wyllie, "New Documentary Light," 460.

[267] Wyllie, "New Documentary Light," 461.

Bibliography

Andrews, Jeanmarie. "Another Famous Ride." *Early American Life* (April 2013): 48-51.

Babits, Lawrence E. and Joshua B. Howard, *Long, Obstinate, and Bloody: The Battle of Guilford Courthouse*. Chapel Hill: The University of North Carolina Press, 2009.

Breig, James. "Williamsburg Moves to Richmond." *The Journal of the Colonial Williamsburg Foundation* 35, no. 2 (2013): 52-59.

"Brigadier General Thomas Nelson Jr." in U. S. National Park Service, *Yorktown Battlefield*. Last updated July 31, 2014. http://www.nps.gov/york/historyculture/nelsonjrbio.htm

Britton, Rick. "From Cuckoo to Charlottesville: Jack Jouett's Overnight Ride," *Journal of the American Revolution* (March 5, 2013), http://allthingsliberty.com/2013/03/from-cuckoo-to-charlottesville-jack-jouetts-overnight-ride/.

------. "Midnight rider: How Jack Jouett saved Virginia," *The Hook* no. 1019 (May 12, 2011). http://www.readthehook.com/90493/overnight-ride-jack-jouett's-race-cuckoo

Capt Christopher Hudson tombstone. http://www.findagrave.com/cgi-bin/fg.cgi?page=gr&GRid=59868369.

Carson, Jean, *Patrick Henry, Prophet of the Revolution*. Williamsburg: Virginia Independence Bicentennial Commission, 1979.

Conrad, Bryan. "Lafayette and Cornwallis in Virginia, 1781." *William and Mary College Quarterly Historical Magazine, 2nd series* 14, no. 2 (1934): 99-104.

Cooper, Jean L., *A Guide to Historic Charlottesville and Albemarle County Virginia*. Charleston: The History Press, 2007.

Crews, Ed. "Captain Jack Jouett's Ride to the Rescue." *The Journal of the Colonial Williamsburg Foundation* 28, no. 3 (2006): 66-71.

Cummins, Joseph, *Ten Tea Parties: Patriotic Protests that History Forgot*. Philadelphia: Quirk Books, 2012.

Dabney, Virginius. "From Cuckoo Tavern to Monticello." *The Iron Worker* 30, no. 3 (1966): 1-10.

------. "Jack Jouett's Ride." *American Heritage Magazine* 13, no. 1 (1961): 56-59. http://americanheritage.com.

------. "Jouett Outrides Tarleton." *Scribner's Magazine* 83 (1928): 690-698.

------. *The New Dominion*. New York: Doubleday & Company, 1971.

Davis, Curtis Carroll, ed. "Farewell to Fleming! Lewis Littlepage Eulogizes a Patriot." *The Virginia Magazine of History and Biography* 74 (1966): 448-451.

Evans, Emory G., *Thomas Nelson of Yorktown; Revolutionary Virginian*. Charlottesville: University of Virginia Press, 1975.

Ewald, Captain Johann, *Diary of the American War: A Hessian Journal*. Translated and edited by Joseph P. Tustin, New Haven, CT: Yale University Press, 1979.

Fleming, Thomas, *What If? Watersheds, Revolutions, and Rebellions, Unlikely Victory*, Robert Cowley, ed. New York: Simon and Schuster Audioworks, 2000: Tape 1 b.

Grayson, Jennie Thornley, *Jack Jouett of Albemarle: The Paul Revere of Virginia*. Charlottesville: Daughters of the American Revolution, Jack Jouett Chapter, 1922.

Hirschfeld, Fitz, ed. "Burnt All Their Houses." *The Virginia Magazine of History and Biography* 99, no. 4 (1991): 513-530.

Hudson, Christopher. "Deposition of Christopher Hudson." *William and Mary Quarterly Historical Magazine, 2nd series* 20, no. 1 (1940): 113.

Hudson, Rector. "Christopher Hudson Insures Thomas Jefferson's Safety." *Tyler's Quarterly Historical and Genealogical Magazine* 22 (1940): 97-105.

Jouett, Edward S. "Jack Jouett's Ride." *Filson Club Historical Quarterly* (1950): 142-157.

Kindig, Thomas, "Benjamin Harrison, 1726-1791." *Signers of the Declaration of Independence*. c2009-2014. http://www.ushistory.org/declaration/signers/harrison.htm; and *Wikipedia.org*, s.v. "Benjamin Harrison V."

Kranish, Michael, *Flight from Monticello: Thomas Jefferson at War*. New York: Oxford University Press, 2010.

Loth, Calder, ed., *Virginia Landmarks Register*. Charlottesville: University of Virginia Press, 1986.

Maass, John R. "To Disturb the Assembly." *Virginia Cavalcade* 19, no. 4 (2000): 149-158.

------. "To Disturb the Assembly: Tarleton's Charlottesville Raid and the British Invasion of Virginia. 1781." *A Student of History*. http://fusilier.wordpress.com/banastre-tarleton-article-2000/

Malone, Dumas, *Jefferson the Virginian*. Boston: Little, Brown and Company, 1948.

------. *Thomas Jefferson: A Brief Biography*. Charlottesville: Thomas Jefferson Memorial Foundation, Monticello Monograph Series, 1933.

Mattern, David B., *Benjamin Lincoln and the American Revolution*. Columbia: University of South Carolina, 1995.

Mapp, Alf J., Jr., *Thomas Jefferson, A Strange Case of Mistaken Identity*. New York: Madison Books, 1987.

McCue, Edward O., III, *A Jouett Miscellany* unpublished notes. Albemarle and Charlottesville, Virginia Historical Society (March 1981): 1-8.

McDowell, Bart, *The Revolutionary War; America's Fight for Freedom*. Washington D.C.: National Geographic Society, 1967.

McLaughlin, Jack, *Jefferson and Monticello: The Biography of a Builder*. New York: Holt Paperbacks, 1990.

Moran, Donald Norman, ed. "Jack Jouett of Virginia the 'Other Ride.'" *The Valley Compatriot* (February 1984). http://americanrevolution.org/jouett.html.

Morgan, Robert, *Boone: a Biography*. Chapel Hill: Algonquin Books, 2008.

"Mourning Glenn Harris," *Leanne Cragun's Family History*. http://www.cragun.com/leanne/getperson.php? personID=I688&tree=Dalling.

Nelson, James L., *George Washington's Great Gamble*. New York: McGraw-Hill, 2010.

Palmer, William P., ed., *Calendar of Virginia State Papers*, vol. 3, 4, 9. New York: Kraus Reprint Corp., 1968.

Pawlett, Nathaniel M. and Howard H. Newlon, Jr., *The Route of Three Notch'd Road: A Preliminary Report*. Rev. ed. (Richmond, VA: Virginia Department of Transportation, 2003). http://www.virginiadot.org/VTRC/main/online_reports/pdf/76-r32.pdf

Rucker, Ambrose. [*Will of Ambrose Rucker*.] Transcribed and posted online by Jo Thiessen. 1996. http://familytreemaker.genealogy.com/users/p/h/e/Mark-Phelps-NC/FILE/0081page.html.

Sackville King's Ordinary. https://sites.google.com/site/kinggenealogy/sackvilleking%27sordinary. Last revised July 14, 2014.

Selby, John, *The Revolution in Virginia 1775-1783*. Williamsburg: The Colonial Williamsburg Foundation, 1988.

Tarleton, Banastre, *A History of the Campaigns of 1780 and 1781, in the Southern Provinces of North America*. London: T. Cadell, 1787.

"Trinity Church," *Little Bits of History Along U.S. Roadways*. http://littlebitsofhistory.blogspot.com/2012/12/trinity-church.html.

"Walker, John, (1744-1809)," in *Biographical Directory of the United States Congress, 1774 to the present*. http://bioguide.congress.gov/scripts/biodisplay.pl?index=w000059.

Ward, Harry M. and Harold E. Greer, Jr., *Richmond during the Revolution 1775-83*. Charlottesville: University Press of Virginia, 1977.

Woods, Edgar, *Albemarle County in Virginia*. Charlottesville: The Michie Company Printers, 1901.

Wyllie, John Cook. "Daniel Boone's Adventures in Charlottesville in 1781 some Incidents Connected with Tarleton's Raid." *The Magazine of Albemarle County History* 19 (1960-61): 1-17.

------. "New Documentary Light on Tarleton's Raid." *Virginia Magazine of History and Biography* 74, no. 4 (1966): 452-461.

------. "Writings about Jack Jouett and Tarleton's Raid on Charlottesville." *The Magazine of Albemarle County History* 17 (1958-1959): 46-56.

Wikipedia sites:

Cary, Archibald.
http://en.wikipedia.org/wiki/Archibald_Cary.

Convention Army.
http://en.wikipedia.org/wiki/Convention_Army. Last updated May 2009.

Government of Virginia.
http://en.wikipedia.org/wiki/Government_of_Virginia.

Harrison, Benjamin.
http://en.wikipedia.org/wiki/Benjamin_Harrison.

Henry, Patrick.
http://en.wikipedia.org/wiki/Patrick_Henry.

Hessian (soldiers).
http://en.wikipedia.org/wiki/Hessian_%28soldiers%29.

Jouett, Jack.
http://en.wikipedia.org/wiki/Jack_Jouett.

Kinloch, David.
http://www.royalprovincial.com/military/rhist/britlegn/blcav1.htm

Kinloch, Francis (Congressman).
http://en.wikipedia.org/wiki/Francis_Kinloch_%28Congressman%29.

Lee, Richard Henry.
http://en.wikipedia.org/wiki/Richard_Henry_Lee.

Nelson, Thomas, Jr.
http://en.wikipedia.org/wiki/Thomas_Nelson,_Jr.

Phillips, General William.
http://en.wikipedia.org/wiki/William_Phillips_%28British_Army_off
icer%29.

Rock Castle (Virginia).
http://en.wikipedia.org/wiki/Rock_Castle_(Virginia). Last revised
June 5, 2013.

Stevens, General Edward.
http://en.wikipedia.org/wiki/Edward_Stevens_%28general%29.

Tyler, John, Sr.
http://en.wikipedia.org/wiki/John_Tyler,_Sr.

Virginia General Assembly.
http://en.wikipedia.org/wiki/Virginia_General_Assembly.

Index

Jack Jouett: Revolutionary Rider

121

Jack Jouett: Revolutionary Rider

ISBN 978-1-4675-9030-3

9 781467 590303

90000>

CPSIA information can be obtained
at www.ICGtesting.com
Printed in the USA
BVOW06s1850030417
480182BV00012B/55/P